10 Performance-Based STEM Projects

Grades 4–5

10 Performance-Based STEM Projects

Todd Stanley

Routledge
Taylor & Francis Group
NEW YORK AND LONDON

First published in 2018 by Prufrock Press Inc.

Published 2021 by Routledge
605 Third Avenue, New York, NY 10017
2 Park Square, Milton Park, Abingdon, Oxon OX14 4RN

Routledge is an imprint of the Taylor & Francis Group, an informa business

Cover and layout design by Allegra Denbo

ISBN 13: 978-1-0321-4217-3 (hbk)
ISBN 13: 978-1-6182-1796-7 (pbk)

DOI: 10.4324/9781003232520

TABLE OF CONTENTS

INTRODUCTION

Why Project-Based Learning?

When my assistant principal, Dr. Jones, would visit my science and social studies class and observe the project-based learning (PBL) my students were engaged in, he would always ask in the post-conference, "How do you know it is working?" To me, this seemed like asking someone why water is wet. It just is. Through the day-to-day observations, I could see that my students were more engaged and learning more through project-based learning than the traditional teaching methods I had used during the first 5 years of my teaching career. Were their test results better at the end of the year? Yes, but more important than this quantitative data was the qualitative data my students provided me. My students would come to visit me after having left for high school and say, "High school is easy because we used project learning in your class. I knew how to research, I knew how to present, and I remembered the material we learned." When students and their parents would talk about their later schooling experiences, they were always grateful we had done project-based learning because it better prepared them for the future.

Despite these stories, Dr. Jones would always resist: "Where's the research to back up that this is working in the classroom?" This was right at the beginning of the data explosion in education, and I did not have any research to tell me it was working. I just *knew* it was working. Again, Dr. Jones would challenge me: "If you had research to back this up, it

DOI: 10.4324/9781003232520-1

would make the power of its effectiveness much better because it would be quantifiable."

Since these conversations, project-based learning has been slowly but surely making its way into the educational conversation. Documentaries such as *Most Likely to Succeed* (Dintersmith & Whiteley, 2015) show the power PBL can have on students. As PBL has gained traction in schools, there has been more and more research on its effectiveness. Not only did I know it was working, but I could also back it up with study after study.

How Effective Is Project-Based Learning?

When Thomas (2000) reviewed research on PBL, he found evidence that using it in the classroom enhanced the quality of student learning, especially when compared to other methods of instruction. Specifically, he saw that PBL was effective for teaching processes, such as problem solving and decision making. Boaler (2002) looked at two British secondary schools that had a similar student makeup. One of these schools used traditional methods to teach mathematics. The other focused on project-based learning. Across 3 years of data, students in the project-based learning school outperformed the traditional school's students in mathematics, with 3 times as many students scoring the highest possible grade on the national examination (Boaler, p. 16). More than that, PBL better taught conceptual and applied knowledge, meaning there was a much better chance of enduring understanding.

In a more recent study, Deitering (2016) looked at whether project-based learning was a more effective instructional method than traditional teaching methods. She compared two groups, one taught through PBL and one taught through more traditional methods. Figure 1 summarizes her findings. Each group completed a science unit on rocks and erosion, followed by a reflection, which required students to consider three levels of engagement—retreatism, compliance, and engagement. The results of the student surveys showed that traditional instruction resulted in better student compliance. When students sit in perfectly positioned rows and are talked *at* for great lengths, it only makes sense that they would be compliant. Traditional methods were also higher in retreatism, but this is not a good thing. Retreatism is when students are disengaged from current classroom activities and goals. Although they are compliant, they are thinking about other things, causing them to reject both the official goals

	Controlled Group Traditional Instruction	Experienced Group PBL Instruction
Retreatism	7%	2%
Compliance	24%	11%
Engagement	44%	82%

FIGURE 1. Traditional instruction versus project-based learning in the classroom and student-reported levels of engagement (Deitering, 2016).

and the official means of achieving the goals of the classroom. When it comes to engagement, PBL wins by a bunch. Eighty-two percent of students said PBL methods were engaging to them, while less than half said the same thing about traditional classroom methods. When you add it all up, compliance may be nice, but it does not mean students are learning.

The Buck Institute for Education (n.d.), which is one of the biggest proponents of PBL, has found that:

- **PBL engages hearts and minds:** Through active engagement, PBL provides real-world relevance for learning, as students solve problems that are important to them and their communities.
- **PBL provides deeper learning:** PBL builds deeper understanding and retention.
- **PBL provides exposure to adults and careers:** Students can interact with mentors in their communities and develop career interests.
- **PBL provides a sense of purpose:** Seeing the real-world impact of a project gives students a greater sense of purpose.
- **PBL builds 21st-century workplace skills:** Students learn to take initiative and responsibility, solve problems, and communicate ideas.
- **PBL provides rewarding teacher-student relationships:** Teachers, too, discover meaning and rediscover the joy of learning while working with students engaged in PBL.
- **PBL engages creativity and technology:** Students use a variety of approaches and technology tools throughout the course of their projects.

What Is Effective Project-Based Learning?

A literature review by MDRC (Condliffe, 2017) described PBL as "promising but not proven" (p. iii). Notably, however, Condliffe did not find overwhelming evidence of PBL's effectiveness. This is because not all PBL is created equally. Just because someone claims to be "doing PBL" in his or her classroom does not mean he or she is doing so with the best practices in mind (p. 20). There are certain elements needed for effective PBL, including (Menzies, Hewitt, Kokotsaki, Collyer, & Wiggins, 2016):

> 1. Student support: pupils need to be effectively guided and supported through the PBL process; emphasis should be given on effective time management and student self- management including making safe and productive use of technological resources.
> 2. Teacher support: regular support needs to be offered to teachers through regular networking and professional development opportunities. Support from the school senior management is crucial.
> 3. Effective group work: high quality group work will help ensure that pupils share equal levels of agency and participation.
> 4. Balancing didactic instruction with independent inquiry will ensure that pupils develop a certain level of knowledge and skills allowing them to comfortably engage in independent work.
> 5. Assessment emphasis on reflection, self, and peer evaluation: evidence of progress needs to be regularly monitored and recorded.
> 6. An element of student choice and autonomy throughout the PBL process will help pupils develop a sense of ownership and control over their learning. (pp. 10–11)

These elements all need to be in play as you utilize project-based learning in the classroom. As you dive into the projects in this book, you will find they are well laid out for you, but there are certain things that you will have to independently ensure are accomplished, such as managing students, giving them enough space to learn how to learn, and giving them guidance on how to reflect upon what they have learned (Stanley, 2015).

When all is said and done, I know my students are learning much more in my project-based learning classroom than when I was teaching with traditional methods. And now I have the research to back that up. How do you like that, Dr. Jones?

Why STEM?

STEM (science, technology, engineering, and math) education is much more than the mashing together of these subject areas. In this book, students will utilize STEM principles to engage in project-based learning through performance-based projects. These projects will involve:

- Designing, developing, and utilizing technological systems
- Open-ended, problem-based design activities
- Cognitive, manipulative, and effective learning strategies
- Applying technological knowledge and processes to real world experiences using up-to-date resources
- Working individually as well as in a team to solve problems (International Technology and Engineering Educators Association, 2016, para. 3)

Typically, students utilizing STEM principles to engage in PBL will:

- Access and synthesize prior knowledge in science, math, and technology to solve a real-world problem
- Research and collect evidence to solve a problem
- Gain firsthand experience on how science, math, and technology solve problems in the real world
- Conceptualize, build, and test concrete models of solutions
- Work collaboratively to critique and build on their peers' ideas
- Communicate and defend solutions based on evidence (Advancement Courses, 2015, para. 3)

STEM-based PBL provides students with authentic learning experiences. Through such experiences, students understand the context of how what they are learning fits into the real world. This means that students are better equipped to apply a concept or skill in a later project or unit, as well as when they go on to college or enter the workforce. By developing authentic products and solving real-world problems, students are able to experience and see firsthand how classroom concepts work in real-world settings. By utilizing STEM principles, they are also able to see how concepts connect across subject areas.

Traditionally, students might work on math for 45 minutes. Then, the bell rings, and the math books and work go away, only to be replaced by science books and assignments. When the bell rings again, everything students have been learning about is put on hold, and they transition into learning about something else. This is a very unnatural way to learn about science and math—and any other subject, for that matter. Math and science are subject areas that are very close cousins, with a lot of overlap between the two of them. Why do we try so hard to separate them?

Anyone who lives in the real world knows this is not how it works. Oftentimes, you employ several different areas of learning while working on a single project. For example, the simple act of making dinner uses several disciplines:

- **English language arts:** Reading the recipe or the directions for preparing the meal.
- **Math:** Measuring out what is needed to create the meal and using a timer to determine how long it should cook.
- **Science:** Understanding when water is boiling, an oven is warmed, or what to mix and what not to mix together to get the desired results.

By completing almost any task, you integrate different subject areas to be able to achieve a goal. That is the way our lives work, and it is how classrooms should work as well. If the STEM education initiative has done anything, it has taught teachers and students how all of these areas work together and how they can be used collectively to achieve a greater accomplishment than if using a single subject area.

You can also use STEM-based PBL to engage students in the engineering design process (Engineering is Elementary, 2018). See Figure 2 for a breakdown of the process. This five-step cycle (ask, imagine, plan, create, improve) is the same process real-world engineers utilize. This is a sound process that can even be applied to subjects unrelated to science, technology, engineering, or math.

For example, if you have asked students to write an essay on what their favorite color is, they could easily go through these steps in order to complete their task:

- **Ask:** Students ask and consider, "What is my favorite color?"
- **Imagine:** Students ask and consider, "Why is it my favorite color?"
- **Plan:** Students ask and consider, "How could I explain to others why it is my favorite color, and what examples could I use?"
- **Create:** Students write their essays.
- **Improve:** Students read through their essays, looking for clarity, as well as spelling and grammar errors.

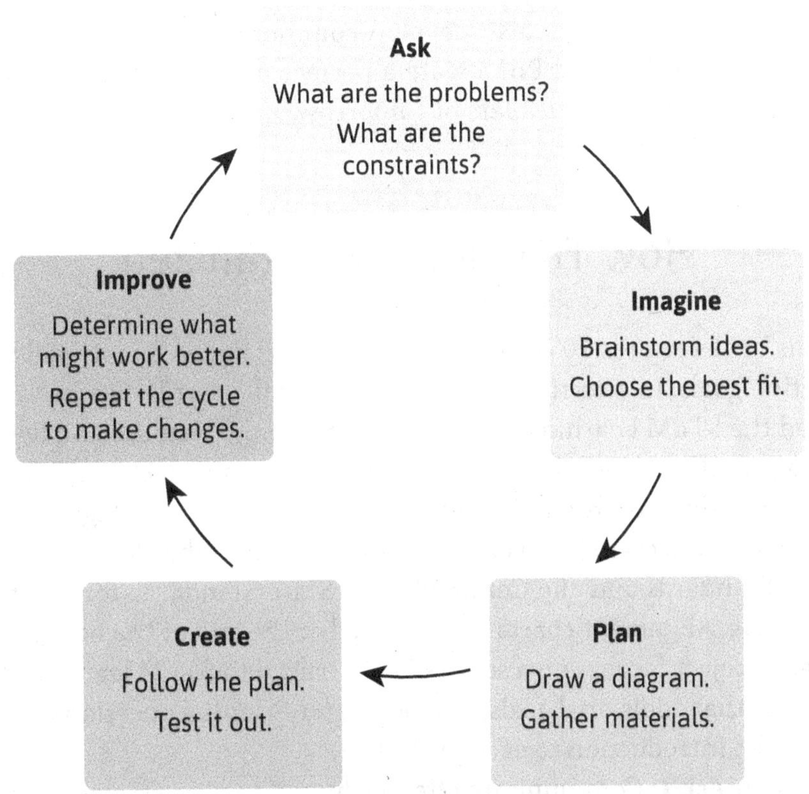

FIGURE 2. Engineering design process. Adapted from Engineering is Elementary, 2018.

The engineering design process gives students a good, solid model to follow, which can be applied throughout STEM areas as well as to social studies, art, and even gym class. Once students are familiar with the engineering design process, they will intrinsically revert to it whenever they are working on something. This is the true value of STEM learning.

Why STEM and PBL?

STEM-based PBL naturally lends itself to the formation of 21st-century skills, which are crucial to students' development in school and beyond. STEM learning engages students and equips them with critical thinking, problem-solving, creative, and collaborative skills. Because of the authentic nature of STEM-based PBL experiences and the final products that students create, students also develop communication skills as well as self-direction. STEM and PBL create a perfect marriage in ensuring students are ready to be the leaders of tomorrow.

How This Book Is Organized

This book features 10 projects. Each project is linked to national STEM education goals. In selecting projects and the skills that they emphasize, I utilized the STEM Learning Goals and the System Dynamics and Systems Thinking Tools and Learning Strategies that make up effective STEM education, according to Creative Learning Exchange (2016; see Figure 3), as a framework. Projects are also based on and aligned to the Next Generation Science Standards and the Common Core State Standards for the target grade levels. Alignment charts are provided at the end of the book.

Each project focuses on a selected skill crucial to STEM learning; however, note that additional goals, big ideas, and essential questions are outlined in the introduction to each project:

- **Project 1:** Communicate effectively.
- **Project 2:** Focus on inquiry and collaboration.
- **Project 3:** Understand multiple content areas.
- **Project 4:** Explore contemporary issues.
- **Project 5:** Use technology, math, and reasoning.
- **Project 6:** Use and analyze models.
- **Project 7:** Record and analyze data.
- **Project 8:** Investigate change over time and patterns.
- **Project 9:** Use computer models or simulations.
- **Project 10:** Construct and explain systems.

Using System Dynamics and Systems Thinking (SD/ST) Tools and Learning Strategies to Build Science, Technology, Engineering, and Math Excellence

One of the hardest areas of the STEM curriculum and, in fact, all curriculum, is creating the context for students to gain experience and practice in the process of critical thinking. The utilization of SD/ST offers a unique methodology for addressing these higher-order thinking skills in a way that creates a framework to gain knowledge, as well as the tools to communicate thought. SD/ST offers an integrated way of thinking, in practical and useful ways, about the systems that surround us, and how they change over time.

☐ Science, Technology, Engineering, and Mathematics Learning Goals

■ System Dynamics and Systems Thinking Tools and Learning Strategies

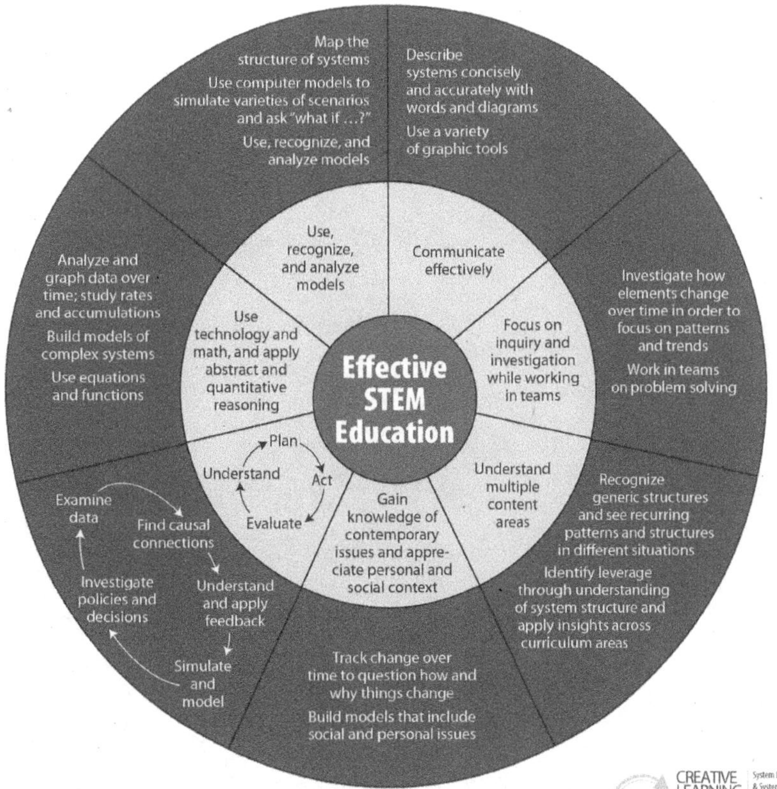

Creative Learning Exchange · Working in K-12 education to develop Systems Citizens
27 Central Street, Acton, MA 01720 978-635-9797

CREATIVE LEARNING Exchange — System Dynamics & Systems Thinking in K-12 Education
www.clexchange.org

FIGURE 3. Effective STEM education. From "Using System Dynamics and Systems Thinking (SD/ST) Tools and Learning Strategies to Build Science, Technology, Engineering, and Math Excellence," by Creative Learning Exchange, 2016, retrieved from http://www.clexchange.org/curriculum/standards/stem.asp. Copyright 2016 by Creative Learning Exchange. Reprinted with permission.

1 Communicate Effectively

The ability to communicate effectively—both verbally and in writing—is crucial to our students during their time in our classrooms and beyond. Consider a lawyer. He has to be able to write legal briefs that enable him to build his case. He also needs to communicate these briefs to the judge or court in order to effectively represent his clients. Doctors also use a combination of these skills. They have to be able to communicate effectively with their patients in order to explain what is going on, and they have to record what they learned into patients' files so that there is an established record of patients' health. These are simplified examples, but that does not diminish the importance of communication skills.

Teachers, especially, utilize communication in their profession, from teaching concepts to a class, to communicating with parents, administrators, and other stakeholders, and more. If a teacher is effectively going to provide feedback to students, he or she must be able to convey this feedback both in written and verbal form. This double reinforcement better equips students to learn from mistakes and strive for improvement in the future.

What does communication look like in a STEM project? It can take a variety of forms, depending on the product that students are asked to produce. For example, if students have been charged with defending a pro-

DOI: 10.4324/9781003232520-2

posal for a design for a product they wish to market to an authentic panel, they will have to employ their speaking skills in order to effectively communicate their plan. Such a presentation requires a combination of style and substance—style in the manner in which the proposal is presented and substance in the quality of the information presented. Characteristics of high-quality presentations of this nature might include:

- The presentation can be clearly heard the entire time, and the participant speaks slowly and clearly throughout.
- The presenter's demeanor is professional throughout. It sounds as though the presentation has been rehearsed several times.
- The presentation is organized in a manner that makes it easy to follow and to understand what is going on at any given time.

If, however, students were charged with creating a brochure that conveyed the information for the project, they would have to communicate in written form. Characteristics of high-quality products of this nature might include:

- The brochure has little to no spelling/grammatical errors.
- The brochure is typed in a format that makes it easy to view.
- The brochure uses sentence structures that make the paragraphs flow and easy to read.

No matter which style students are asked to communicate in, the substance needs to have the same quality. These descriptors could be used for either written or spoken products:

- The project is organized clearly, allowing someone to know what is being discussed at any given time.
- The student provides plenty of examples to back up statements made.
- The student provides much detail, explaining concepts and ideas so that someone can gain a full understanding of what is being talked about.

It is important that any project you present to students requires them to utilize both written and spoken skills so that students display competence in any venue. This will make them that much more effective when going out in the real world to find themselves a job. After all, the top job skills that companies are looking for in new hires all have to do with communication (Graduate Management Admission Council, 2018; see Figure 4). If you were to help your students master both written and verbal com-

1. Oral communication	6. Value opinions of others
2. Listening skills	7. Integrity
3. Adaptability	8. Follow a leader
4. Written communication	9. Drive
5. Presentation skills	10. Cross-cultural sensitivity

FIGURE 4. Top 10 skills sought by employers. Adapted from Graduate Management Admission Council, 2018.

munication, they would have an advantage over other potential hires who are less accomplished with these skills.

Magnetic English

In this project, students will create a system that allows others to write their own poetry, much like the popular magnetic poetry kits that allow users to rearrange word magnets to write poems. Students' systems should have instructions and prompts in place to help users who may not know a lot about poetry. Users should also have a wide variety of words and phrases to choose from and be able to easily rearrange them to edit and revise their poems.

Students' poetry systems could be as simple as words written largely on a sheet of paper or words displayed on large building blocks. Students should be as creative as they like, but in the end, people need to be able to use their systems to easily create their own poetry.

Materials

- Magnetic poetry kits (for student use)
- Project Outline: Magnetic English (student copies)
- Suggested Timeline
- Lesson: What Is Poetry?
- Lesson: Lines and Stanzas
- Lesson: Rhythm/Rhyme
- Lesson: Tone and Mood
- Handout 1.1: Poetry Auction (student copies)
- Product Rubric: Magnetic English (student copies)

Name: ______________________ Date: ______________

PROJECT OUTLINE

Magnetic English

Big Idea

Communication can take on many forms.

Essential Question

How can you create a model that allows those who are not poetry writers to construct and communicate their own poems?

Deliverables

You will create a system that allows others to write their own poetry, much like the popular magnetic poetry kits that allow users to rearrange word magnets to write poems. But get creative! Your system should have instructions and prompts in place to help users who may not know a lot about poetry. Users should also have a wide variety of words and phrases to choose from and be able to easily rearrange them to edit and revise their poems.

Constraints

Your system must feature prompts and well-written instructions.

SUGGESTED TIMELINE

DAY **1**	**2**	**3**	**4**	**5**
Introduce the project and Conduct Lesson: What Is Poetry? *Ask.*	Conduct Lesson: Lines and Stanzas. *Ask.*	Conduct Lesson: Rhythm/ Rhyme. *Ask.*	Conduct Lesson: Tone and Mood. *Ask.*	Have students complete a poetry auction as a class or in groups (see Handout 1.1). *Imagine.*
6 Have students brainstorm their poetry models. *Plan.*	**7** Have students create their poetry models. *Create.*	**8** Have students create their poetry models. *Create.*	**9** Have students create their poetry models. *Improve.*	**10** Have students demonstrate their poetry models.

LESSON

What Is Poetry?

1. Tell students that, as they may know, poetry is a very beautiful art form. This art form can be displayed through song. Find the lyrics to a current hit song or a favorite song to share with students (or consider having students find songs to share with the class). You can first read the lyrics and then play the song. Discussion questions may include:
    - What do you think the song is about?
    - What feeling does this song convey to you?
    - How does the song use rhyme or rhythm?
    - Do the song lyrics read like a poem, or do you need the music for the lyrics to sound poetic?
    - How does the chorus of the song convey the central meaning of the lyrics?

2. Explain to students that a poem can capture an experience or a feeling through readers' (or listeners') imaginations.
3. Students may ask themselves about the differences between poetry and prose. Explain that there isn't much difference. The lines between the two are very blurred. There can be a poem that is very prose-like, such as *Beowulf*, which tells an entire story in poetic form. Edgar Lee Masters wrote a book of poetry called *Spoon River Anthology* in which each poem is about a different person in the city of Spoon River. The poems can stand alone, but, all together, they tell the story of the town.
4. Explain to students that poetry:
    - tends to be more compressed than prose—you don't need to write as much to convey a poem as you do a prose piece;
    - tends to place more emphasis on *how* something is said and less on *what* is said compared to prose;
    - usually has more rhythm than prose, as well as interesting shape and form;
    - has a less rigid structure than prose, allowing writers to be more experimental and creative; and
    - usually encompasses a feeling and uses sensory language to express that feeling.

5. Explain that, during this project, students will use what they know and what they learn about communicating through poetry to write their own poems, as well as to develop their poetry models.
6. Have students use magnetic poetry sets to write their own poems. Students can share their poems with a partner or read them to the class. Have students discuss what they think others' poems mean and what their poems mean.

LESSON

Lines and Stanzas

1. Explain to students that there are many reasons to write a poem, such as:
   - explaining a moral,
   - telling a story,
   - sketching a scene/character,
   - describing an experience,
   - feeling the joy of language/rhythms,
   - sharing a memory, or
   - sorting out feelings.

2. Tell students that a poem can be about the most intense feeling the writer has ever experienced or about a simple object, such as Charles Simic's "The Spoon."
3. Explain that, in Simic's poem, a spoon has taken on a new meaning. Simic clearly saw the spoon differently than a reader normally would. He personified the spoon.
4. Ask: *What is personification?* (This is when a writer assigns human qualities to something that does not, in reality, have these characteristics.)
5. Have students either choose nonliving objects themselves or have them pull names of objects from a bag/hat. Working in groups or individually, students can write a few lines of poetry that bring the nonliving object to life.
6. Afterward, tell students: *There are many other poetic devices used in Simic's poem, including tone, stanza breaks, metaphors, and line breaks. These elements all help with the structure of a poem.*
7. Explain that a poet's subject potentially determines how he or she sets up a poem.
8. Explain that poems are typically divided up into lines. Some poems have set patterns where all the lines are the same length, while others have lines that vary in length. There are no rules for line length, but sometimes a poet may try to accomplish something with different line lengths, such as a concrete poem, which is constructed in a shape that matches the poem's topic. Consider "A Christmas Tree" by William Burford.
9. Have the class look at one or more concrete poems. Then, ask students: *But what decides line length in poems that are not shaped like an object?* Usually there are two ways to determine line length: by meaning and by syllable. Tell students that it can be easier to break lines by syllable because a poem is more likely to flow and develop a pattern. If a poet chooses to break lines by meaning, inventiveness is the key to successful breaks.

10. Consider "Triad" by Adelaide Crapsey. The syllable pattern is 2, 4, 6, 8, 2. This structure is known as cinquain. Tell students that writing lines in which the pattern emphasizes certain key words requires a lot of thought and frequent editing.
11. Explain that the Japanese haiku is another form of breaking lines by syllables. Ask: *Does anyone know what a haiku is?* A haiku has a 5-7-5 syllable count. In addition to the syllable count, haikus usually (1) have a reference to nature, (2) describe a particular event, (3) are set in the present, and (4) have a mystical quality.
12. Have students practice trying to write haikus. They can share these with a partner or with the class.
13. Afterward, explain to students that some poets always write in stanzas, while others do not. How this is decided depends on the sense of the poem. Stanzas have special names depending on the number of lines (e.g., two lines = couplet, three lines = tercet, four lines = quatrain, etc.). There is structure to poetry, but this structure can be played with.

LESSON

Rhythm/Rhyme

1. Tell students that when many people think of poetry, they think of rhyming. Rhyming can help with the rhythm and flow of poetry, but it is not necessary. Share with students a rhyming poem, such as "Do Not Go Gentle Into That Good Night" by Dylan Thomas. Ask students: *What's the pattern in this poem?* The first and third line of every stanza all rhyme, and the middle line from every stanza rhyme (i.e., ABA ABA ABAA).
2. Bring in a collection of Dr. Seuss books. Working in groups, students should go through a couple of pages of a few Dr. Seuss titles and determine what each book's rhyming pattern is. Have groups report their findings to the rest of the class.
3. Tell students: *If you are going to rhyme, there should be a pattern of some sort. But the pattern is really up to you. The rhyming words do not need to be one syllable. The trick to good rhyming is to be inventive.* Ask students to think of some examples of rhyming words with more than one syllable (e.g., innocent and meant, and hyperbole and be).
4. Say: *There are also near-rhymes, where the words don't exactly rhyme, but they still sound sort of the same.* Ask students to think of some examples of near-rhymes (e.g., asleep and eat, shoes and moot, stand and man, etc.).
5. Remind students that it is not necessary to rhyme in poetry. There are ways of finding rhythm in poetry without rhyme. Consider alliteration. Ask: *Does anyone know what alliteration is?* It is the repetition of initial sound or the same letter. Share with students some examples of alliteration (e.g., *write* and *real*, *knob* and *nail*, etc.).
6. Tell students that most of modern poetry does not rhyme but is lyrical. William Carlos Williams, a famous poet, never rhymed, but his poems were very lyrical (e.g., "To an Elder Poet"). The lyrical characteristics add to the poem's rhythm.
7. Have students try to write poems without rhyming (they can use the magnetic poetry sets).
8. Explain that rhythm is very important to poetry. Say: *Just as if you feel your pulse and you get a pattern, rhythm is the blood flow of poems. Words have a rhythm to them based on their sounds. Songs have rhythm to them. Ballads are a form of poetry that are very song-like.* Share with students an example, such as "Casey at the Bat" by Ernest Lawrence Thayer.
9. Explain that the smallest unit you can break a word into is a syllable. Some syllables naturally become loud (are stressed), and others soft (are unstressed), which adds to rhythm. There are also fast and slow rhythms in poetry. Ask students: *If*

a poem feels fast, what kind of feeling is it trying to evoke? (Excitement, energy.) *If a poem is slow, what feeling is it trying to evoke?* (Tranquility, relaxedness.) To make a line run slowly, a poet uses more stressed syllables and shorter words. To speed up the rhythm, a poet uses fewer stressed syllables and longer words.

LESSON

Tone and Mood

1. Tell students that poetry is a method of communication. It is important that poets clearly indicate their attitude toward the subject of their poem. If they are talking about something serious, poets don't want their readers to think that they are being funny and vice versa. This is why tone is important.
2. Say: *When writing poetry, consider the best way to communicate what you are writing about. Should you be humorous . . . detached . . . passionate? In communicating tone, you have to be careful about the words that you choose. The choice of words can easily suggest an attitude. This suggestive factor is called connotation.*
3. Explain that mood can also give a poem a feeling. Mood is derived from the attitude of the author toward his or her subject. A poem sets its mood with its images, its details, and its words. Have students consider a poem like "The Flower Boat" by Robert Frost. Ask: *What mood does this poem portray?* (It evokes pleasant feelings; it is optimistic.)
4. Share a few techniques that can be used in building tone and mood:
   - Having more stressed sounds per line creates a slower, more dignified effect. Rhythms and meters having more unstressed sounds usually create a lighter, quicker effect.
   - Certain sounds have a harsh or soft tone. Letters such as K and G have a harsh tone. L, M, and N, on the other hand, are much softer. B, T, and P are explosive sounds.
   - The images a poet uses to convey the experience will suggest his or her attitude or create a mood. This is the most important technique.
   - Poems can be of various lengths (there is no rule). However long a poem is, the language of poetry is the language of compression. Poets say as much as they can as quickly and cleanly as possible.

Name: ______________________________ Date: ____________________

HANDOUT 1.1

Poetry Auction

Directions: Going once . . . going twice . . . prepare for a poetry auction! You will write an opening line to a poem. Then, you will share this opening line with the class or a group. Other students will offer suggestions—or bids—for the next line. As bids come in, you will collect new lines for your poem and compile them into a final work.

1. Write your opening line.

2. Why does your line work as an opening line? Describe the poem you imagine following your opening line. Consider how many lines and stanzas it will have, as well as its rhyme scheme, rhythm, mood, tone, etc.

3. Read your opening line to the class and discusses its possibilities.

4. Other students will begin making bids, offering suggestions for the next line. As the author, you will continue collecting bids until you have the lines of your choosing to build a poem that you feel does your opening line justice.

Name: ______________________________ Date: ______________

Handout 1.1: Poetry Auction, *continued*

5. Record your final poem here or on a separate sheet of paper.

6. Now bid on others' work until the auction is over!

Note. This activity is adapted from Waters, 1992.

Name: ______________________ Date: ______________

PRODUCT RUBRIC

Magnetic English

	Usability	The Evidence
Great	There are clear directions for using the poetry model. Users can easily shift words to edit and revise their poems. There is a wide variety of words for users to utilize.	There are prompts provided that inspire users to create a poem. The poetry model is creative in its use of materials and how it works. The model looks professionally made; words are spelled out correctly and neatly written.
Good	There is a set of directions for using the poetry model, but the instructions are not always clear. Users are able to shift words so that they can edit and revise their poems for the most part, but the model could be more user-friendly. There is a variety of words for users to utilize.	There are prompts provided, but they are not particularly inspiring. The poetry model is simple in its use of materials and how it works. The model looks professionally made; most words are spelled out correctly and/or neatly written.
Needs Improvement	There is not a set of directions for using the poetry model; it is confusing and difficult to use. Users are not able to easily shift words to edit and revise their poems. There is a limited amount of words for users; it is difficult for users to find what they need.	There are no prompts provided, or they do not make any sense. The poetry model is inappropriate in its use of materials; it is difficult to work with. The model does not look professionally made; many words are misspelled and/or sloppily written.

2 Focus on Inquiry and Collaboration

Students should be engaging in inquiry on a daily basis. Through inquiry, students discover things for themselves, much like they did when they were young children first learning about their place in the world. Inquiry is what caused them to first discover what got their parents' attention or first emulate another person's actions. Oftentimes the inquiry came from experimenting with something and, if it did not work, learning from mistakes.

The best way to facilitate an environment of inquiry in the classroom is through teaching students to ask the right sorts of questions. Younger students, especially, may need more guidance as to what form these questions will take. And the subject matter students are inquiring about should be rather subjective. If you get into a discussion about what color the sky is, the answer is always going to come down to blue. If, however, you have a more open-ended inquiry, such as what brand of pizza is best or whether it is ever okay to lie, the conversation is going to be endless because there is no correct answer.

Fostering inquiry is what the engineering design process (see Figure 2) is all about. In each and every step, students discover new ideas and concepts for themselves. When they start, they are discovering the problems

DOI: 10.4324/9781003232520-3

and constraints by asking questions. They then come up with ideas and a plan, letting their imaginations run wild. The next step involves experimenting with materials and what it will take to make students' ideas come alive. Finally, students look at what they have done and try to make it better, inquiring as to what this might look like.

Part of this process is also having the ability to fail. Failure used to have such a negative connotation in education. Failing a class meant you were not doing well. Now there is a new outlook on failure. Fail actually stands for "first attempt in learning." There should be a space in the classroom where students can make mistakes without fear. This should especially be present during the improve phase of the engineering design process, where students must weigh what has worked, what has not, and figure out how to make the product better. The only way they are going to be able to do this successfully is if they can mess up in the first place.

The ability to work in a group and collaborate is a valuable 21st-century skill that is important to teach, even to young children. Students need to know how to resolve differences with classmates, divvy up tasks amongst peers, and produce something together they would have been unable to produce by themselves. Teachers cannot just put them into groups and hope for the best.

One way to ensure that students are working well together is to give each an individual role that will help the group. This way, instead of five people all trying to take charge, each person has a specific area to specialize in, which will make the quality of the product that much better. If each group member focuses on his or her job, the product the group creates should be better than if any member had worked on it on his or her own. There will likely need to be some conversation about the roles. For example, just making a student the leader might not be enough for him or her to succeed in that role. There might need to be a discussion about what a good leader does. Other roles should also be clearly laid out. If there is room for interpretation, it is best to have a discussion as a class as to what the role should look like.

Once students have been given these roles, there is clear accountability. If something was not written down, it is the scribe who is responsible for it. If a direction was left out of the final product, the quality controller should have caught it. This accountability takes out that mob mentality where everyone in the group is held equally accountable. Even though students are given specific tasks, however, it is important for them to see how collaborating enabled them to develop a better product together.

Pumpkin Catapult

In this project, students will work in groups to design and build a working catapult. They will then test and experiment with their catapults, working to refine and make any improvements to their products. Groups will present their completed catapults in a competition on the final day of the project. Whichever catapult is able to throw a 1-pound pumpkin the farthest will be the winner. Students' catapults will be evaluated on the distance the pumpkin travels, not on how pretty or professional the catapult looks.

Note. You will need to procure an outside space in order to test the catapults. At all times, ensure students are practicing good safety procedures.

Materials

- Supplies for class catapult (see Lesson: Building a Class Catapult)
- Supplies for student catapults (dependent upon student-selected designs)
- Project Outline: Pumpkin Catapult (student copies)
- Suggested Timeline
- Lesson: What Is a Catapult?
- Lesson: Building a Class Catapult
- Handout 2.1: Designing Your Catapult (student copies)
- Handout 2.2: Catapult Testing (student copies)
- Product Rubric: Pumpkin Catapult (student copies)

Name: ____ Date: ____________________

PROJECT OUTLINE

Pumpkin Catapult

Big Idea

Designing and redesigning a device can make it as effective as possible.

Essential Question

How can you build and then improve a design?

Deliverables

You will work in a group to design and build a working catapult. You will then test and experiment with your catapult, working to refine and make any improvements to your product. You and your group will present your completed catapult in a competition on the final day of the project. Whichever catapult is able to throw a 1-pound pumpkin the farthest will be the winner. Your catapult will be evaluated on the distance the pumpkin travels, not on how pretty or professional the catapult looks.

Members of your group will take on the following roles:

- **Engineer:** Responsible for overseeing the design of the catapult.
- **Quartermaster:** Responsible for making sure that the materials that are needed to build the catapult are procured.
- **Test pilot:** Responsible for testing the catapult and overseeing improvements that need to be made.
- **Project manager:** Responsible for overseeing the entire project and making sure the group meets its deadlines.
- **Foreman:** Responsible for overseeing the construction of the catapult.

Note. Practice safety at all times. Do not test catapults indoors. Do not aim catapults at anyone else.

Constraints

Your catapult must:

- be able to throw a pumpkin that weighs approximately 1 pound, and
- work on its own to throw an object.

SUGGESTED TIMELINE

DAY **1** Introduce the project and conduct Lesson: What Is a Catapult? *Ask.*	**2** Conduct Lesson: Building a Class Catapult. *Ask.*	**3** Divide students into groups and have students brainstorm ideas for their catapults (see Handout 2.1). *Imagine.*	**4** Have students brainstorm ideas for their catapults. *Imagine.*	**5** Have students determine materials for their catapults. *Plan.*
6 Have students design their catapults. *Plan.*	**7** Have students design their catapults. *Plan.*	**8** Have students design their catapults. *Plan.*	**9** Have students begin constructing their catapults. *Create.*	**10** Have students construct their catapults. *Create.*
11 Have students construct their catapults. *Create.*	**12** Have students test their catapults (see Handout 2.2). *Improve.*	**13** Have students revise their catapults. *Improve.*	**14** Have students make final changes to their catapults. *Improve.*	**15** Have groups demonstrate their catapults and determine the best catapult.

LESSON

What Is a Catapult?

1. Explain that a catapult is a machine used to throw objects over a great distance. Catapults use weights and levers to launch objects, and they were commonly used in the Middle Ages as weapons.
2. Explain that students are going to create catapults that can launch pumpkins. There are pumpkin chucking (or punkin chunkin) competitions across the United States, in which participants build catapults to launch pumpkins. The current world record is about 5,500 feet (Guinness World Records, n.d.)—just more than a mile.
3. Share with students some examples of pumpkin catapults, such as:
   - "The Physics of 'Punkin Chunkin'" (available at https://www.youtube.com/watch?v=sXuQvAPwcOE)
   - "Pumpkin Chuckin World Record" (available at https://www.youtube.com/watch?v=MtKyCrfmlnA)
   - "Punkin Chunkin 2011" (available at https://www.youtube.com/watch?v=HhjmgLJwebY)
   - "How to Build a Trebuchet | MythBusters" (available at https://www.youtube.com/watch?v=9-Hwxw4fgqk)
   - "Pumpkin Catapult" (available at https://video.nationalgeographic.com/video/us_catapultpumpkins)
4. Be sure to explain that students' catapults will be much smaller in scale than the videos they have watched, but the videos give students a general idea of how catapults work.

LESSON

Building a Class Catapult

1. Tell students that, as a class, you are going to make a miniature catapult to give students an idea of what they will be doing as they embark upon this project. The class catapult, which can either be constructed by the teacher or by having students work in small groups, only needs to be able to launch a cotton ball, while students' catapults will have to be able to launch a 1-pound pumpkin. Explain that, for this reason, students will not be able to use the exact same design as the class catapult. They will need to modify the design and/or research other designs in order to be able to construct a catapult to launch a pumpkin.
2. A video of catapult-building instructions is available at https://www.youtube.com/watch?v=iKQaTFfhwWo. Written directions for building a simple catapult are available at https://www.scientificamerican.com/article/build-a-catapult.
3. Make sure you demonstrate correct safety procedures as you build the class catapult.
4. After the catapult is constructed and you have tested launching cotton balls, have students reflect. Ask:
   - Was the catapult a success? Why or why not?
   - How could we have improved the catapult?
   - Are there different materials we might have considered using?
   - What would need to be done to this catapult to enable you to launch a larger object like a pumpkin?
   - What are some things we need to do in order to ensure that everyone is safe with this project?

Name: ______________________________ Date: ______________

HANDOUT 2.1

Designing Your Catapult

Directions: In order to design your own catapult, you and your group members first need to work together to select a design. You are more than welcome to research ideas on the Internet and select a design you believe will be the most successful.

When you have selected the design you want to use, you must draw a plan so that you know how you are going to put it together. Your plan should include:

- measurements,
- materials that will be used, and
- how the catapult will be constructed.

Tips for Creating a Catapult Design

- Use graph paper, or design the catapult on a computer.
- Use proper drawing tools (e.g., a ruler, a compass, etc.).
- Use a pencil for the initial drawing and then go over it with pen.
- Show more than one angle if that helps in visualizing the catapult.
- Include dimensions for the model (i.e., how many inches/feet long or wide each part will be).
- Label the different parts of the design, writing clearly in print.
- Make the design recognizable enough for others to tell what it is.

Building the Catapult

- Once the design is completed, your team will need to decide who will bring in what materials or work with your teacher to acquire them.
- You will also need to figure out if you need any tools in order to construct your catapult.
- The building process should be completed during class.

Name: ______________________________ Date: ______________

HANDOUT 2.2

Catapult Testing

Directions: Today you will test and improve your catapult.

1. Conduct multiple tests. Record the distance your catapult is able to throw an object. You will want to practice with an object such as a softball (which can be a little less messy than a pumpkin!).

2. From these tests, you will want to determine if any improvements need to be made to your catapult. You may need to make the structure studier, create more torque on the arm, reconsider the angle from which you are launching, build a better vessel for holding/throwing your pumpkin, or lengthen the swinging arm of the catapult

Test	Distance Object Was Thrown	Improvement(s) Made to Catapult
1		
2		
3		
4		
5		

Name: ______________________________ Date: ______________

PRODUCT RUBRIC

Pumpkin Catapult

	Design/Model	Effectiveness	Group Work
Excellent	Design clearly shows how the catapult will be built; measurements and parts are labeled. Model looks somewhat like the design, but effective improvements have been made.	Catapult is able to effectively throw the pumpkin; the distance thrown is above average compared to other groups. It is clear where improvements were made. Catapult is easy for the team to use.	Student made him- or herself a valuable member of the group, offering positive contributions to the group dynamic. Student contributed to his or her part of the experiment as well as others.
Good	Design shows how the catapult will be built; most measurements and parts are labeled. Model looks somewhat like the design, but improvements have been made (although not always effectively).	Catapult is able to throw the pumpkin fairly effectively; the distance thrown is average compared to other groups. Improvements were made to improve its effectiveness, but they are not clear. Catapult can be used by the team but not always easily.	Student made him- or herself a valuable member of the group most of the time by offering positive contributions to the group dynamic. Student contributed to his or her part of the experiment but not many others.
Needs Improvement	Design does not show how the catapult will be built; few to no measurements and parts are labeled. Model looks nothing like the design, and/or there have not been any significant improvements made to increase effectiveness.	Catapult is not able to throw the pumpkin very well, and/or the distance thrown is below average compared to other groups. It is unclear where improvements were made. Catapult cannot be used by the team, or it is very difficult to use.	Student did not contribute positively to the group dynamic; he or she was often a negative distraction. Student did not adequately contribute to his or her part of the experiment.

3 Understand Multiple Content Areas

Once in the real world, students have to be able to pull different skills learned in separate arenas and put them together. Different subjects and skills work together to get desired results. What if schools facilitated more opportunities for students to build crosscurricular skills? STEM education is a perfect example of combining subject areas. Many educators include art in STEM education, known as STEAM. Others, still, include reading (STREAM), as there are connections to English language arts and literacy across the curriculum, such as writing a research paper, reading for comprehension, or conducting an interview. The sooner you expose students to a crosscurricular model, the better, as crosscurricular learning results in more authentic learning. Through crosscurricular lessons and activities, students can better understand the context of what they are learning and how it fits into the real world.

You know crosscurricular learning is working when students are utilizing skills from various subject areas—perhaps without even realizing the connections at first. If students are writing a research paper on the importance of various modes of transportation, such as the railroad, steamboats, and national roads, they may not realize they are learning about history while doing so or, alternatively, might not realize they are using language

DOI: 10.4324/9781003232520-4

arts skills to learn about history. Or, during a science project involving the creation of a new version of a mousetrap, students may not realize the math skills they are developing by drawing a plan with dimensions.

The advantages to this integrated learning for students are many. A comprehensive study on "The Logic of Interdisciplinary Studies" (Mathison & Feeman, 1997) discovered that students experienced:

- an increase in understanding, retention, and application of general concepts;
- a better overall comprehension of global interdependencies, along with the development of multiple perspectives, points of view, and values;
- an increase in the ability to make decisions, think critically and creatively, and synthesize knowledge beyond the disciplines;
- the increased ability to identify, assess, and transfer significant information needed for solving novel problems;
- the promotion of cooperative learning;
- a better attitude toward the self as a learner and as a meaningful member of a community; and
- increased motivation (pp. 19–20).

Integrated approaches make learning more organic and less forced. As human beings we are natural learners. From the moment we are born, we are learning every single second through experience. And yet, in school, we often take these experiences away and try to make what is being taught rigid and artificial. By using integrated learning, we allow students to experience how these subject areas all work together in the natural order of things. When learning is more natural, so are the results.

Strands of the Same DNA

In this project, students will explore the close relationship between science and mathematics. They will select a science topic of interest to them (or, at your discretion, related to a current topic being covered in class). The project is broken into four parts:

- **Part 1:** Students will research the relationship between math and their science topic. They will write a three-paragraph paper summarizing their findings or create a slideshow with a minimum of four slides. They will document their sources and include a bibliography.

- **Part 2:** Students will create a visual model to represent their topic. This can be computer generated, a video-recorded demonstration, or a physical model created out of a medium of their choice. The options are endless. The model can be no larger than one square meter in size. It may be as small as an 8 ½ by 11-inch piece of paper.
- **Part 3:** Students must conduct an interview with an expert related to their scientific topic about how the expert uses math in his or her everyday tasks. This interview can be completed any time during the project. This can be an expert in the field (e.g., an engineer, meteorologist, architect, veterinarian, etc.). Students need to let the teacher know as soon as possible if they need help finding someone to interview. Students can conduct an in-person, phone, e-mail, or video chat (e.g., FaceTime, Skype) interview. Questions for the interviewee need to be approved by the teacher before the interview is conducted. Students must ask at least five questions.
- **Part 4:** Students need to decide on a final project that brings all of the components together in a presentation. Product options include a written paper, visual presentation (such as a slide presentation, trifold poster, Nearpod lesson, Prezi, Kahoot, website, etc.), skit, or other product. The visual model (photo of product or video of demonstration embedded in final product), interview findings and reflections on what was learned, research, and bibliography will be included in the final product. The presentation should be no more than 15 minutes and no fewer than 10 minutes.

Materials

- Project Outline: Strands of the Same DNA
- Suggested Timeline
- Lesson: Math and Science Connections
- Handout 3.1: Recording Research
- Handout 3.2: Conducting an Interview
- Product Rubric: Math and Science Connections
- Product Rubric: Scientific Model
- Product Rubric: Strands of the Same DNA Final Presentation

Name: ______________________ Date: ______________

PROJECT OUTLINE

Strands of the Same DNA

Big Idea

Math and science are closely related.

Essential Question

How do science and math work together?

Deliverables

In this project, you will explore the close relationship between science and mathematics. You will select a science topic of interest to you. The project is broken into four parts:

- **Part 1:** You will research the relationship between math and your science topic. You will write a three-paragraph paper summarizing your findings or create a slideshow with a minimum of four slides. You will document your sources and include a bibliography.
- **Part 2:** You will create a visual model to represent your topic. This can be computer generated, a video-recorded demonstration, or a physical model created out of a medium of your choice. The options are endless. The model can be no larger than one square meter in size. It may be as small as an 8 ½ by 11-inch piece of paper. You will eventually exhibit your model and elicit feedback from fellow students.
- **Part 3:** You must conduct an interview with an expert related to your scientific topic about how the expert uses math in his or her everyday tasks. This interview can be completed any time during the project. This can be an expert in the field (e.g., an engineer, meteorologist, architect, veterinarian, etc.). You need to let the teacher know as soon as possible if you need help finding someone to interview. You can conduct an in-person, phone, e-mail, or video chat (e.g., FaceTime, Skype) interview. Questions for the interviewee need to be approved by the teacher before the interview is conducted. You must ask at least five questions.
- **Part 4:** You need to decide on a final project that brings all of the components together in a presentation. Product options include a written paper, visual presentation (such as a slide presentation, trifold poster, Nearpod lesson, Prezi, Kahoot, website, etc.), skit, or other product. The visual model (photo of product or video of demonstration embedded in final product), interview findings and reflections

Name: ______________________ Date: ______________

Project Outline: Strands of the Same DNA, *continued*

on what was learned, research, and bibliography will be included in the final product. The presentation should be no more than 15 minutes and no fewer than 10 minutes.

Constraints

Your project should clearly demonstrate the relationship between science and math.

SUGGESTED TIMELINE

DAY				
1 Introduce the project and conduct Lesson: Math and Science Connections.	**2** Have students conduct research to find science topics they are interested in learning more about. *Ask.*	**3** Have students continue conduct research, finalizing their topics by the end of the day. *Ask.*	**4** Have students begin more in-depth research, learning all they can about their topics. *Imagine.*	**5** Have students continue to research their topics. *Imagine.*
6 Have students continue to research their topics. *Imagine.*	**7** Have students continue to research their topics. *Imagine.*	**8** Have students begin writing their papers or completing their slideshows (Part 1). *Plan.*	**9** Have students continue writing their papers or completing their slideshows (Part 1). *Plan.*	**10** Have students complete their papers or slideshows (Part 1). *Plan.*
11 Have students begin working on their models (Part 2). *Plan.*	**12** Have students work on their models (Part 2). *Create.*	**13** Have students work on their models (Part 2). *Create.*	**14** Have students work on their models (Part 2). *Create.*	**15** Have students exhibit their models.
16 Have students begin planning their presentations (Part 4), including their interviews (Part 3). *Improve.*	**17** Have students continue planning their presentations (Part 4). *Imagine.*	**18** Have students work on their presentations (Part 4). *Create.*	**19** Have students work on their presentations (Part 4). *Create.*	**20** Have students present their projects.

LESSON

Math and Science Connections

1. Explain to students that science and math are closely related to one another. They will often find math concepts in science topics. Ask: *Can anyone think of any examples?* Guide students to make connections, such as:
    - **Chemistry:** Using data in a table.
    - **Meteorology:** Measurement of temperature and humidity.
    - **Geology:** Using coordinates.
    - **Botany:** Measuring the width and length of trees and plants.
    - **Engineering:** Measurement and use of shapes.

2. Provide students with a more in-depth example. Tell students that math is also used a lot in the science of astronomy, the study of space. An example of this would be determining the length of time that it takes for planets to orbit the sun: Earth takes approximately 365 days to orbit the sun. As a result, one year is 365 days long. However, other planets take less or more time to orbit around the sun, which means a year on another planet might be shorter or longer than that on Earth.
3. Explain that Venus orbits the sun in just 225 days. That is 140 days less than on Earth. For every year old a person is on Earth, he or she would be approximately a year and a half older on Venus. If a person is 12 years old on Earth, he or she has lived 4,380 days (i.e., 12 years × 365 days). On Venus, this person would be 19.5 years old (i.e., 4,380 ÷ 225).
4. Have students determine how many years old they would be on other planets, using the approximate number of days it takes each planet to orbit the sun:
    - Mercury: 88 days
    - Mars: 687 days
    - Jupiter: 4,333 days
    - Saturn: 10,755 days
    - Uranus: 30,687 days
    - Neptune: 60,190 days

5. Students have just explored one way in which math can be applied in the field of astronomy. Tell students that, in this project, they will need to pick a scientific field of interest to them and explore how math is used in that field. Perhaps that field is astronomy, computer science, chemical engineering, medicine, veterinary science, marine biology, etc. Whatever topic students choose, remind them that in order to complete the project, they will need to interview an expert in that field.

Name: ______________________________ Date: ______________

HANDOUT 3.1

Recording Research

Directions: For Part 1 of the project, you have two options for how you wish to summarize your findings. You may either (1) write a three-paragraph paper or (2) create a slideshow with a minimum of four slides. Use this handout to record and organize your thoughts and research.

Introduction (Paragraph 1 or Slide 1)

Hook:

Background Points:

Thesis Statement:

Body (Paragraph 1 or Slide 2)

Topic Sentence:

Supporting Fact 1:

Supporting Fact 2:

Name: ______________________________ Date: ______________

Handout 3.1: Recording Research, *continued*

Conclusion (Paragraph 3 or Slide 3)

Restatement of Thesis:

Summary of Main Points:

Challenge to the Reader:

Bibliography (End of Paper or Slide 4)

Name: ______________________________ Date: ______________

HANDOUT 3.2

Conducting an Interview

Directions: Your interview can be conducted anytime during the 4 weeks of the project. The interview can either be completed face-to-face or via phone, e-mail, or video chat. You are responsible for finding your interviewee. You might consider friends of your parents, parents of your classmates or friends, local businesses, universities, or conducting an Internet search for a worthy expert.

The interview should be completed in three steps:

1. **Set up the interview.** This will involve making a call, sending an e-mail, or somehow making contact with the person you are interviewing:
   - Make sure you tell the interviewee why you are contacting him or her and what you hope to get out of the interview.
   - Make sure you agree on a time and, if applicable, a place.
   - Be professional and polite at all times.
   - If you are leaving a message, repeat your name and phone number twice to ensure the person received it.

2. **Conduct the interview.** Remember that your goal is to learn how this person uses math in his or her everyday job:
   - Know your stuff. The only way to develop good questions is to research and know as much information as possible about your subject.
   - From your research, create a list of five or more questions. The more specific your questions are, the better. Don't ask questions that can be answered with a simple "yes" or "no" unless that is the answer you are looking for. Make your interviewee talk and explain.
   - Write all of your questions down. Have your teacher approve them. Then practice asking them. Become very familiar with your questions before you go into the interview. This will allow you to ask follow-up questions as you converse with your interviewee.
   - Be prepared. Bring a pencil, notebook, recorder, and/or your questions. Always ask permission before recording an interviewee. Be prepared to take notes even if you are recording the conversation.
   - Be on time. Arrive at your interview with plenty of time to spare. There is nothing more unprofessional than showing up late after asking someone to give up his or her time.

Name: ______________________________ Date: ______________

Handout 3.2: Conducting an Interview, *continued*

- Be polite to your subject. Make eye contact. Always take time to ask for an explanation about things you don't understand. Don't be afraid of uncomfortable silences and pauses, and let the interview take its natural course.
- Always listen carefully to the answers. Each answer could lead to more questions or include an answer to a question you haven't asked yet. Don't read through your questions one right after another like a list. Conduct your interview like a conversation.

3. **Debrief.** After the interview, expand your notes by following up on things you learned in your interview with more research. Review your research and your interview notes. Circle or highlight quotations that you think will help you with your project.

Interview Questions

Question #1: ______________________________

____

Question #2: ______________________________

____

Question #3: ______________________________

____

Question #4: ______________________________

____

Question #5: ______________________________

____

Name: ______________________ Date: ______________

PRODUCT RUBRIC

Math and Science Connections

	Math/Science Connections	Essay	(Optional) Slides
Excellent	Clear and detailed connections are made between how math and science are used in the topic; connections are explained and illustrated with several examples. A bibliography is included and shows that research came from multiple sources.	Essay follows the three-paragraph structure and outline in detail. Essay establishes a thesis and supports it with evidence. Writing features correct spelling, grammar, and sentence structure throughout.	Slides provide a clear overview of math and science connections. Slides follow the outline, establishing a thesis and supporting it with clear evidence. Slides are visually pleasing and look professional. Writing features correct spelling and grammar.
Good	Connections are made between how math and science are used in the topic, but could be explained more clearly. More examples could be used to illustrate connections. A bibliography is included and shows research came from one or two sources.	Essay follows the three-paragraph structure and outline, but it lacks detail in some areas. Essay establishes a thesis but does not always support it with evidence. Writing features correct spelling, grammar, and sentence structure with just a few mistakes.	Student includes a minimum of four slides but could have included more details. Slides follow the outline, establishing a thesis but could have included clearer evidence. Slides are visually pleasing and look professional. Writing features correct spelling and grammar with just a few mistakes.

Name: ______________________ Date: ______________

Product Rubric: Math and Science Connections, *continued*

	Math/Science Connections	Essay	(Optional) Slides
Needs Improvement	No connections are made between how math and science are used in the topic. Examples are not included to illustrate connections. A bibliography is not included, or it shows research only came from one source.	Essay does not follow the basic three-paragraph structure. Essay does not establish a clear thesis and/or does not support it with any evidence. Writing features poor spelling, grammar, and sentence structure.	Student does not include a minimum of four slides and/or does not show the relationship between math and science. Slides do not follow the outline; a clear thesis is not included and/or there is little to no supporting evidence. Slides are not visually pleasing and look unprofessional. Writing features many spelling and grammar mistakes.

Name: ______________________________ Date: ______________

PRODUCT RUBRIC

Scientific Model

	Object	Display
Great	Model captures the math involved in the science, showing how the two work together. Model is clearly labeled or has a caption explaining with detail the math and science involved.	It is clear which scientific topic the model conveys. Model looks professional, like something one would see in a museum display. Model is no larger than 1 square meter in size or no smaller than an 8 ½ by 11-inch sheet of paper.
Good	Model captures the math involved in the science, but does not clearly show how the two work together. Model is labeled or has a caption explaining the math and science involved, but the connections could be clearer.	It is somewhat clear which scientific topic the model conveys. Model looks semi-professional, like something a high school student would produce. Model is a little larger than 1 square meter in size or a little smaller than an 8 ½ by 11-inch sheet of paper.
Needs Improvement	Model does not capture the math involved in the science and/or does not show how the two work together. Model is not labeled or lacks a caption explaining the math and science involved, making connections unclear.	It is unclear which scientific topic the model conveys. Model does not look professional; it looks thrown together. Model is much larger than 1 square meter in size or much smaller than an 8 ½ by 11-inch sheet of paper.

Name: ____________________ Date: ____________

PRODUCT RUBRIC

Stands of the Same DNA Final Presentation

	Object	Display
Great	Presentation can be clearly heard/seen the entire time, and the presenter speaks slowly and clearly throughout. The presentation is well organized; it easy to follow and understand what is going on at any given time. The presentation is between 10 to 15 minutes in length.	Display provides a complete overview of the research, comparing how the science and math work together. Display shows the model and explains clearly how it demonstrates the relationship between science and math. Display shares experiences from the interview, including reflections, such as lessons learned and perspective gained.
Good	Presentation can be clearly heard/seen, and the presenter speaks slowly and clearly for the most part. Presentation is organized in an easy-to-follow manner; it is easy to understand what is going on most of the time. Presentation is a couple of minutes shorter or longer than the 10- to 15-minute range.	Display provides an overview of the research, comparing how the science and math work together, but there are aspects that are left out that would help with understanding. Display shows the model, including the connection between science and math, but it does not explain clearly their relationship to one another. Display shares a basic overview of the interview but does not adequately include reflections.

Name: ______________________________ Date: ______________

Product Rubric: Strands of the Same DNA Final Presentation, *continued*

	Object	Display
Needs Improvement	Presentation cannot be heard/seen in several instances, and/or the participant does not speak slowly and clearly throughout, making it difficult to understand. Presentation is not very organized, making it difficult to follow and understand what is going on at any given time. Presentation is several minutes shorter or longer than the 10- to 15-minute range.	Display provides a scattered overview of the research, but it does not make it clear how the science and math work together. Display shows the model but does not explain the connection between science and math. Display shares a basic overview of the interview but does not include reflections.

4 Explore Contemporary Issues

Students learn reading, writing, and arithmetic, but we also hope that they will learn to be better people during their time in school. This starts by having awareness—first of those immediately around them. We can grow students' awareness by teaching them to be polite and considerate of their classmates, teachers, and other school community staff through character education. Then, this immediate environment can be expanded to include the community that they live in. What are the town's problems? What can students do to help or contribute more to their community? This grows and grows, expanding to their country and then, ideally, to global awareness.

Global awareness means more than being aware of current events going on around the world. According to the Partnership for 21st Century Skills (2016), global awareness entails:

- Using 21st century skills to understand and address global issues
- Learning from and working collaboratively with individuals representing diverse cultures, religions and lifestyles in a spirit of mutual respect and open dialogue in personal, work and community contexts

DOI: 10.4324/9781003232520-5

- Understanding other nations and cultures, including the use of non-English languages (p. 2)

Global awareness helps students to understand and appreciate personal and social context. Personal context refers to the intrapersonal environment that shapes an individual's experience. Such environmental factors play a role in determining the student's response to experiences and interactions. If a person is prejudiced against someone else or another group or culture, it is probably due to an experience or something that was relayed to him or her that caused such a response. People do not choose to be prejudiced; rather their intrapersonal environment often shapes them into being that way. Social context is recognizing that sometimes your own personal context and that of those around you are not necessarily the same. As an example, this has come up in the news recently: Personal tweets authored by public figures many years ago when they were younger and less aware of the social context of their comments are coming to light, and these individuals are now facing the repercussions. The lesson here is that your digital footprint is there forever. A comment you once made might have been fine in the personal context of your friends, but once exposed to the public, it can come back to haunt you.

To help students become more aware, expose them to contemporary issues that society is dealing with. This could be something that is happening in your town, a cause that needs support, or a worldwide problem, such as hunger or lack of an education. Showing students that they can make a difference can have an effect on their personal context. They might see something from another point of view or gain an understanding of something they were previously ignorant about.

Community service projects are an excellent way for students to learn about contemporary issues, as well as use the engineering design process to problem solve. Whether gathering canned foods for the local pantry, educating others about the opioid epidemic, raising money for kids with cancer, or trying to create practical solutions for farming in third-world countries, students will gain an awareness of the people in these situations and develop empathy. One thing that can frustrate students, especially younger ones, is feeling like there is nothing they can do about a problem. They hear about children starving in Africa, hurricanes that devastate Puerto Rico, or the homeless people in their town, and empathize with the people who are affected. Helping students to understand how they can help not only makes them aware of the problem, but it also makes them aware of what can be done about it.

An American Quilt

In this project, students will study how immigration has affected the demographics of the United States over the last 100 years. They will create a visual that displays their findings, illustrating the increase or decrease of diversity in the U.S. Their visuals may be displayed using a poster, computer graphic, chart, graph, map, or other form. Students must include a legend that identifies what the various items or symbols on their visuals represent.

Materials

- Student computer and Internet access
- Project Outline: An American Quilt (student copies)
- Suggested Timeline
- Lesson: What Is a Melting Pot?
- Lesson: Wy Do People Immigrate to the United States?
- Lesson: Analyzing Immigration Data
- Product Rubric: An American Quilt (student copies)

Name: ______________________________ Date: ______________

PROJECT OUTLINE

An American Quilt

Big Idea

Diversity is important to the identity of the United States.

Essential Question

How has immigration increased or decreased over the past 100 years?

Deliverables

You will study how immigration has affected the demographics of the United States over the last 100 years. You will create a visual that displays your findings, illustrating the increase or decrease of diversity in the U.S. Your visual may be a poster, computer graphic, chart, graph, map, or other form, as long as it visually represents your project. You must include a legend that identifies what the various items or symbols on your visual represent.

Constraints

You may only use data from the last 100 years.

SUGGESTED TIMELINE

DAY				
1 Introduce the project and conduct Lesson: What Is a Melting Pot? *Ask.*	**2** Conduct Lesson: Why Do People Immigrate to the United States? *Ask.*	**3** Conduct Lesson: Analyzing Immigration Data. *Imagine.*	**4** Have students research U.S. immigration over the past 100 years. *Plan.*	**5** Have students continue to research U.S. immigration over the past 100 years. *Plan.*
6 Have students develop their visuals. *Create/ Improve.*	**7** Have students develop their visuals. *Create/ Improve.*	**8** Have students develop their visuals. *Create/ Improve.*	**9** Have students develop their visuals. *Create/ Improve.*	**10** Have students complete their visuals. *Create/ Improve.*

LESSON

What Is a Melting Pot?

1. It is important for students to understand there is more than one culture in the United States. These cultures are based on religion, politics, nationality, etc. This discussion will spark ideas about how these cultures are collectively viewed across the country.
2. Explain to students that the United States is often referred to as a melting pot. Ask: *What does "melting pot" mean?* Show the classic Schoolhouse Rock video "Great American Melting Pot" (available at https://www.youtube.com/watch?v=5ZQl6XBo64M). Guide students to understand that the "melting pot" metaphor describes how people from many different cultures come together to form one American culture.
3. Ask students: *Are there any problems with this metaphor?* Guide students to understand that there is no single harmonious American culture. People from other countries who immigrate to the United States still retain their own cultures and backgrounds.
4. Another metaphor sometimes used to describe the multicultural society of the United States is a salad bowl. Ask: *How might the United States be like a salad bowl?* The ingredients (Americans) are part of the whole salad (the United States), but they also retain their own shape (their cultures).
5. Ask: *Are there any problems with this metaphor?* Guide students to understand that one criticism of this metaphor is that people may not keep their original culture fully intact over time.
6. Another metaphor that is sometimes used is that America is a giant chocolate chip cookie. Ask: *What do you think might be meant by this?* Guide students to understand that chocolate chips are baked into the cookie, but not mixed so much that they lose their general shape or, in this case, culture.

LESSON

Why Do People Immigrate to the United States?

1. Hold a discussion on the many reasons why people may immigrate to the United States (both in the past and present). Explain that one major reason is freedom. Ask students a few basic questions to start off the discussion, such as:
   - What does the Declaration of Independence say are unalienable rights? (Life, liberty, and the pursuit of happiness.)
   - What freedoms does the First Amendment to the Constitution guarantee? (People have freedom of religion, speech, press, assembly, and petition.)
   - Why did the Pilgrims travel to the New World on the *Mayflower*? (They were seeking religious freedom.)

2. Have students brainstorm other ideas. Listed below are some possibilities to guide the discussion. Include past and current-day examples, in order to link the past to the present. Remind students that they will be studying immigration over a 100-year period.
   - **Opportunity:** The United States has a lot to offer in terms of opportunity. There have been many famous "rags to riches" stories.
   - **Wealth:** The United States is considered a wealthy country. It is a center of economic capitalism. Some countries' economies do not support business and industry. It might be easier to make money in the United States. Also labor laws, such as minimum wage and limits on hours, may prevent workers from being taken advantage of.
   - **Education:** Many people come to the United States because of its education system, specifically college.
   - **Jobs:** Many people move to the U.S. for work opportunities.
   - **Refuge:** Some people get pushed out of their own homes and must come to the U.S. for refuge from war, starvation, etc.

3. Ask: *How many people do you think immigrate to the United States each year?* Have students generate a few guesses. Explain that they will be looking more closely at immigration data in the next lesson.

LESSON

Analyzing Immigration Data

Note. In addition to or in lieu of this lesson's contents, you can find a wealth of U.S. immigration charts, graphs, and other data online, such as those available from the Pew Research Center, available at http://www.pewhispanic.org/2017/05/03/facts-on-u-s-immigrants. This resource is ideal for students to explore individually and/or to utilize for a whole-class discussion.

1. Have students analyze immigration data over the past years (display https://www.immigrationeis.org/sites/default/files/images/charts/immigration_into_us_1.gif to generate ideas). Discussion questions may include:
   - What patterns do you notice about immigration to the United States from this chart?
   - Why do you think that immigration was so low from 1931 to 1950?
   - Over the past 50 years immigration has steadily risen. Why do you think that is?
   - Do you think we have been very friendly to immigrants wanting to come to the United States?
   - What would you predict the number of immigrants from 2011–2020 is going to be? Why do you think that?

2. Have students analyze nationalities of those who have immigrated to the United States (display Table 4 and Table 5 available at https://cis.org/Report/Immigrants-United-States-2007 to generate ideas). Discussion questions may include:
   - Prior to 1980, where did most immigrants come from? Why do you think that is?
   - From 1980 to 2007, where did most immigrants come from? Why do you think that is?
   - Why do you think so many immigrants are from Mexico but not from Canada?
   - Which nationalities have increased steadily over the past 50 years? Why do you think that is?
   - Are there any other patterns that you notice?

3. Display the interactive map available at http://www.pewhispanic.org/2015/09/28/from-ireland-to-germany-to-italy-to-mexico-how-americas-source-of-immigrants-has-changed-in-the-states-1850-to-2013. Discuss with students. Ask them to write about five patterns they notice from looking at the interactive map and how immigration has changed over the years.

Name: ______________________ Date: ______________

PRODUCT RUBRIC

An American Quilt

	Visual	Content	Progression
Excellent	Visual is pleasing to the eye and is easy to read. Visual creatively captures the main idea of immigration and how it has progressed over the years.	The statistics used are all from a reliable source and are accurate. There are more than a dozen nationalities represented by the project.	Visual includes more than 5 years of snapshots to show the progression of immigration. Visual clearly shows the pattern of immigration over the last 100 years.
Good	Visual is pleasing to the eye but is not always easy to read. Visual captures the main idea of immigration and how it has progressed over the years, but it could be more creative.	The statistics used are mostly from a reliable source but not all are accurate. There are 8–12 nationalities represented by the project.	Visual includes 5 years of snapshots to show the progression of immigration. Visual shows the general pattern of immigration over the last 100 years, but it could be clearer in some areas.
Needs Improvement	Visual is not pleasing to the eye; it is difficult to read. Visual does not capture the main idea of immigration and how it has progressed over the years.	The statistics used are mostly from an unreliable source and are often inaccurate. There are 7 or fewer nationalities represented by the project.	Visual includes less than 5 years of snapshots to show the progression of immigration. Visual does not clearly show the pattern of immigration over the last 100 years.

5 Use Technology, Math, and Reasoning

Abstract reasoning can be a challenge for students, especially younger ones. This is because they think very much in concrete terms: this or that, black or white, wrong or right. What does it mean to be an abstract thinker? An abstract thinker:

- can understand and separate context from content;
- is able to understand relationships between events or can connect the dots;
- understands the meaning behind words, situations, and events;
- draws generalizations from a specific set of circumstances; and
- has the ability to compare different situations.

According to Stanley (2018), you might hear an abstract thinker "say, 'I wonder . . .' or 'What if this happened . . . ?' They are able to think about situations that are not there, but other students may only be able to think about what is right in front of them" (p. 173). In the classroom, abstract thinkers:

- are able to use metaphors and analogies with ease;
- can understand the relationship between both verbal and nonverbal ideas;

DOI: 10.4324/9781003232520-6

- possess complex reasoning skills, such as critical thinking and problem solving;
- can mentally maneuver objects without having to physically do it, known as spatial reasoning;
- are adept at imagining situations that have happened or are not actually happening; and
- appreciate sarcasm. (p. 173)

Math has a lot of abstract thinking. Even the act of learning to count has many abstract qualities to it, such as (Scholastic, n.d.):

- **The stable-order rule:** Saying counting words only once and in a consistent order (e.g., "seven, eight, nine . . .").
- **The cardinal rule:** Giving a summary or "how many" total. When starting out, children might have to recount to remember the total, but they eventually learn that the last number counted represents the whole, an abstract concept.
- **The abstraction rule:** Not just numbers can be counted. Any object can be counted, whether it be the number of times bouncing a ball, the number of stuffed animals a child owns, etc. You can also count the lack of an object. If you have a tennis ball can with only two balls in it, you can count the missing ball as one.

Not all students naturally think abstractly. But how do we get them to do so using technology and math? One way to do this is through the use of manipulatives. Manipulatives are "items you can touch and move around that allow a student to count, figure out fractions, discern patterns, and other math tasks" (Stanley, 2018, p. 176). Manipulatives include blocks, shapes, base ten blocks, Unifix cubes, fraction bars, and plastic counting cubes. You can also use technology to create manipulatives. There are several digital manipulatives available for students, such as ST Math, which often requires students to manipulate objects in order to arrive at the correct answer, or visual manipulatives like tangrams, which represent physical objects.

Helping students to think abstractly, or develop outside-the-box thinking, will lead to more creativity and innovation. After all, anyone who thinks inside the box can only produce what is in that box. Those who are thinking outside of it can develop new ideas.

Brainteasing Patterns

In this project, students will create a series of 10 brainteasers that involve patterns. These brainteasers should encourage users to think outside of the box in order to solve them, a skill that most scientists, mathematicians, and engineers need to possess in order to be successful. Students do not have to use the same type of puzzle for all 10 brainteasers. Students may utilize numbers, shapes, colors, sizes, designs, or a combination of strategies, or employ math, science, or other skills in order to develop their puzzles. Their end products will be activity sheets featuring their 10 brainteasers, ideally ordered from easiest to most difficult. Others trying to solve the brainteasers should be able to look for patterns and then make predictions on what will happen in the next brainteaser. The solutions must follow a logical pattern, and students will want to make sure their puzzles are challenging but not impossible. On the final day of the project, students will try to solve each other's puzzles.

Note. Introduce students to solving brainteasers and logic puzzles by having them practice solving Sudoku puzzles. If students have never played before, review the rules with them (see http://www.sudoku.com/how-to-play/sudoku-rules-for-complete-beginners for more information). Share with students a variety of Sudoku puzzle books (or many are available online) for beginners to advanced players and see how students respond to the challenge.

Materials

- Variety of Sudoku puzzles (books or online puzzles)
- Project Outline: Brainteasing Patterns (student copies)
- Suggested Timeline
- Handout 5.1: The Empty Triangle (student copies)
- Handout 5.2: The Empty Triangle Answer Key (student copies)
- Handout 5.3: Raven's Matrices (student copies)
- Handout 5.4: Raven's Matrices Answer Key (student copies)
- Product Rubric: Brainteasing Patterns (student copies)

Name: ______________________________ Date: ________________

PROJECT OUTLINE

Brainteasing Patterns

Big Idea

By analyzing patterns we can make predictions.

Essential Question

How can someone predict an outcome based on previous patterns?

Deliverables

You will create a series of 10 brainteasers that involve patterns. You do not have to use the same type of puzzle for all 10 brainteasers. You can utilize numbers, shapes, colors, sizes, designs, or a combination of strategies, or employ math, science, or other skills in order to develop your puzzles. Your end product will be an activity sheet featuring the 10 brainteasers, ideally ordered from easiest to most difficult. Others trying to solve the brainteasers should be able to look for patterns and then make predictions on what will happen in the next brainteaser. The solutions must follow a logical pattern, and you will want to make sure they are challenging but not impossible. On the final day of the project, you and your classmates will try to solve each other's puzzles.

Constraints

Your brainteasers must follow a logical pattern.

SUGGESTED TIMELINE

DAY				
1 Introduce the project and have students explore Sudoku. *Ask.*	**2** Have students explore empty triangles (see Handout 5.1–5.2). *Ask.*	**3** Have students explore Raven's Progressive Matrices (see Handout 5.3–5.4). *Ask.*	**4** Have students begin brainstorming their brainteasers. *Imagine*	**5** Have students continue brainstorming their brainteasers. *Imagine/Plan*
6 Have students work on their brainteasers. *Plan.*	**7** Have students work on their brainteasers. *Create.*	**8** Have students work on their brainteasers. *Create.*	**9** Have students finalize their brainteasers. *Create.*	**10** Have students try to solve each other's brainteasers.

Name: ______________________________ Date: ______________

HANDOUT 5.1

The Empty Triangle

Directions: Empty triangles are a type of logic puzzle. Here is an example:

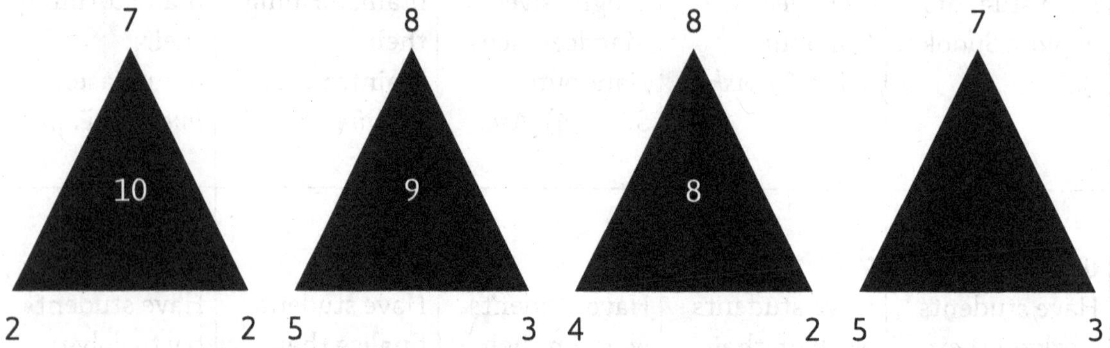

These puzzles require you to determine the relationship/pattern between the other three pyramids and find the missing number for the fourth pyramid. In order to solve this particular puzzle, you take the number at the top and subtract the bottom left number from it: $7 - 2 = 5$.

Then you multiply that number by the bottom right number: $5 \times 2 = 10$ (the number in the center).

Test this pattern on the next two triangles. Then, solve for the center of the fourth triangle (the answer is 6). Now practice this on your own.

Name: ______________________________ Date: ________________

Handout 5.1: The Empty Triangle, *continued*

Problem	Triangle	Top	Center	Bottom left	Bottom right
1.	a	8	11	5	2
	b	5	4	4	5
	c	3	5	7	5
	d	7		2	5
2.	a	6	8	2	4
	b	5	6	3	9
	c	4	8	4	8
	d	4		5	10
3.	a	8	6	4	3
	b	6	9	2	3
	c	9	12	3	4
	d	12		2	3
4.	a	5	6	4	3
	b	4	6	7	5
	c	8	7	8	9
	d	6		8	8
5.	a	6	9	3	2
	b	3	3	5	5
	c	7	7	4	4
	d	5		6	10

Name: ____________________ Date: ____________

HANDOUT 5.2

The Empty Triangle Answer Key

1. 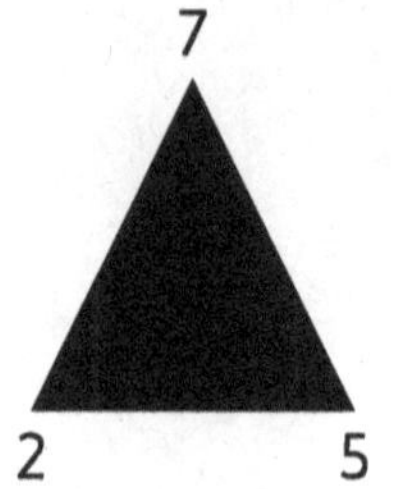

7 + 2 = 9 – 5 = 4

2. 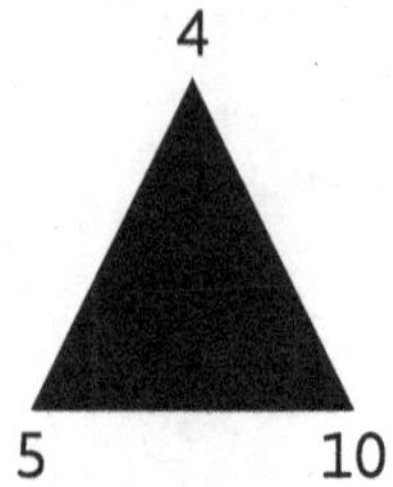

4 × 5 = 20 – 10 = 10

3. 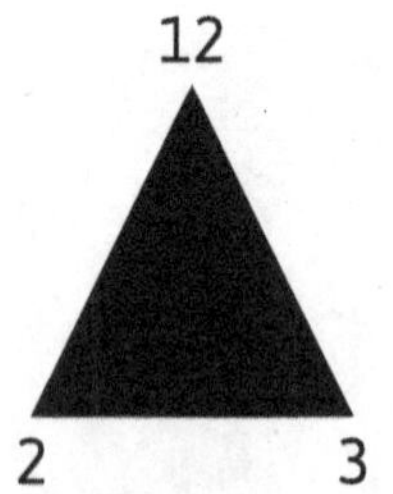

12 ÷ 2 = 6 × 3 = 18

4. 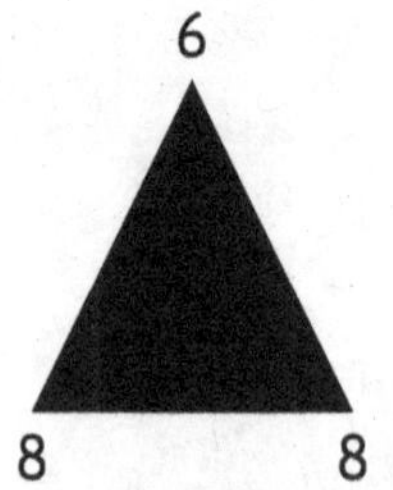

6 + 8 = 14 – 8 = 6

5. 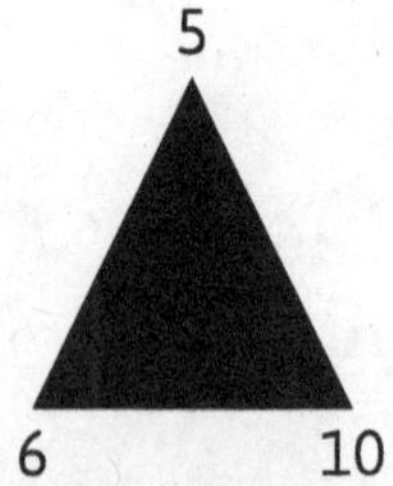

5 × 6 = 30 ÷ 10 = 3

Name: ______________________ Date: ______________

HANDOUT 5.3

Raven's Matrices

Directions: Raven's Progressive Matrices are puzzles that do not even have to involve numbers. They may feature colors, shapes, designs, etc. Here is an example of a cognitive pattern recognition test:

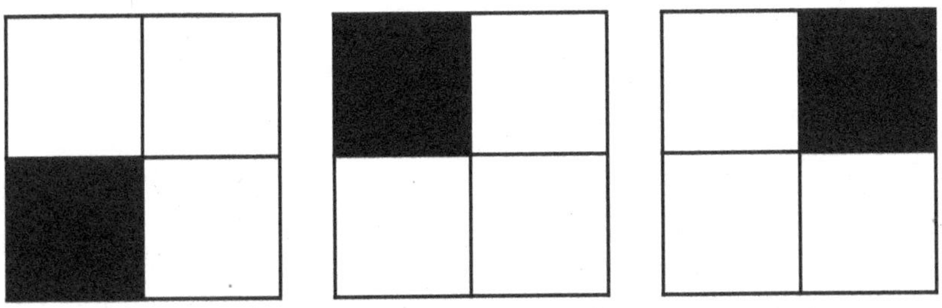

The answer to this puzzle is:

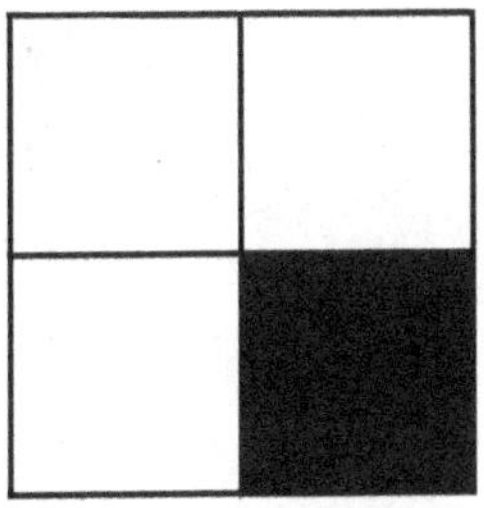

Name: ______________________ Date: ______________

Handout 5.3: Raven’s Matrices, *continued*

Try some more of these puzzles.

1. 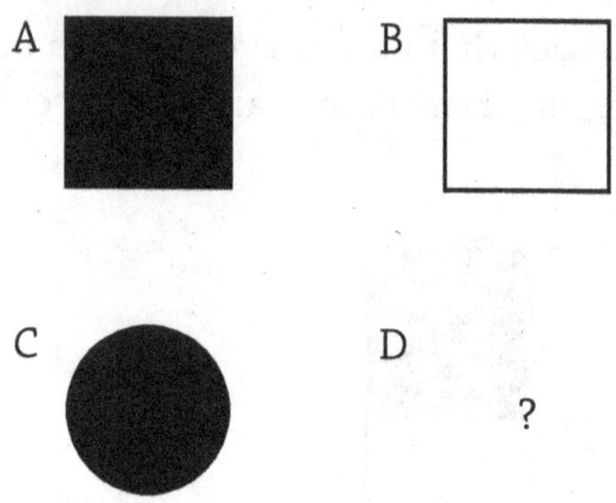

2. 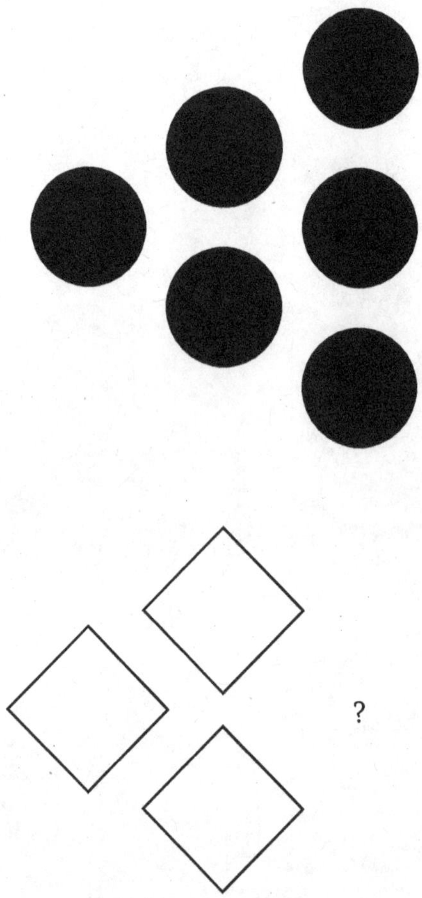

Name: ______________________ Date: ______________

HANDOUT 5.4

Raven's Matrices Answer Key

1. A  B 

C  D 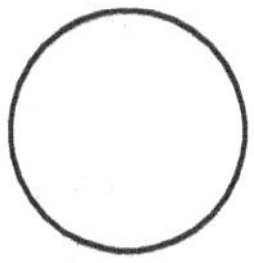

2. 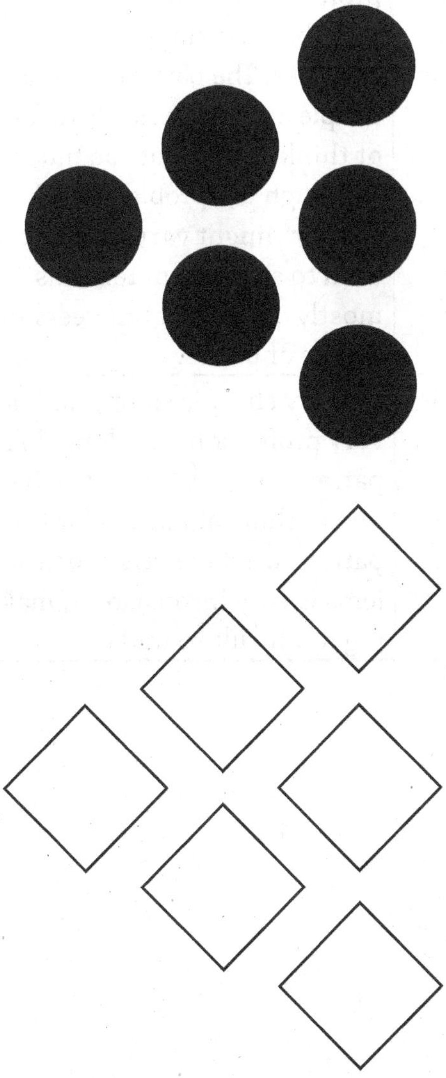

Name: ______________________________ Date: ______________

PRODUCT RUBRIC

Brainteasing Patterns

	Brainteasers	Pattern
Great	Brainteasers are challenging but not impossible to solve. Directions are clear and informative. Student includes more than 10 brainteasers.	Activity sheet is professional-looking and easy to read. The pattern used is clever and requires one to have to think. Although the problems and answers might vary, the pattern used to solve them remains consistent.
Good	Brainteasers are challenging but are too hard or too easy in some areas. Directions are clear for the most part; there is some confusion. Student includes 10 brainteasers.	Activity sheet is mostly professional-looking and easy to read, but it is sloppy in a couple of places. The pattern used is simple and requires a little bit of thinking but not too much. Although the problems and answers might vary, the pattern used to solve them remains mostly consistent but veers in a couple of places.
Needs Improvement	Brainteasers are either too challenging or too easy. Directions are unclear. Student includes fewer than 10 brainteasers.	Activity sheet is sloppy and not very professional-looking. The pattern used does not require one to think at all, and/or the pattern used to solve the problems is very inconsistent, making it difficult to find one.

6 Use and Analyze Models

Models bring ideas and concepts to life, making them more practical and easier to understand. We use models a lot in the STEM world. How many students create their own volcano or make a Styrofoam version of the solar system in science class in order to better understand these concepts? Think about architects and structural engineers. When they develop a new building, they do not build the actual structure at first. They construct a model of it so that they can test it and understand what problems need to be addressed before moving on to the actual structure. A perfect example of this would be the Shanghai World Financial Center. In its first designs and model stage, there was a circular opening near the top of the 1,600-foot tall structure to reduce the stresses of wind pressure. However, when architects created the model, they understood the difficulty and expense of making the shape circular. Buildings typically use straight lines in their construction because they are more practical and easier to work with. Because of this, they changed the shape to that of a trapezoid.

Most importantly, models allow us access that we might not have otherwise. We cannot take a student into the center of Earth in order to experience its layers. Not only is this impractical from the standpoint of getting permission slips and liability waivers, but it is also impossible to

DOI: 10.4324/9781003232520-7

dig that deep or survive the molten outer core of our planet. However, we can analyze a model of the Earth that shows the different layers, helping students to see something they normally would not be able to see. It would also be challenging to take someone's skull off and poke around in his or her brain in order to understand how it works. But a plastic version of the human brain with removable parts allows someone unlimited access to learn about the brain's structure without risk.

Would students rather read about the rainforest in a book or create a version of the biome complete with producers, consumers, and resources? Would students rather look at photos of the Eiffel Tower or create their own out of toothpicks? Wouldn't it be so much more fun to create a model of New York City that shows the coordinate plane rather than sketching out lines on a worksheet? Models make learning both engaging and authentic. Students learn more through such hands-on activities and actually produce something that others are going to see on display.

Analyzing models also leads to greater understanding. Meteorologists study models of hurricanes in order to try to predict what path one might actually take. Mathematicians spend a lifetime studying models, trying to crack the code that will lead to a new mathematical concept. Engineers study models of new cars and how they react to resistance in wind tunnels to shape the final design of the vehicle. When students create models, they can then analyze other students' models to gain a better understanding. Rather than have each student create a model of the human body, have each student take a different part of the human body and create a more detailed model. If you have 20 students in the classrooms, you could have 20 different body parts. When you go to display, set up the classroom like a human body, the brain being at the top, the heart or stomach being in the middle, with the feet being at the bottom. Students can walk around this giant human body, learning about different parts and organs and what they do for the body.

Models are a practical way to study large concepts, and best of all, they bring learning to life. Students are able to interact and study the models so that they see how abstract concepts actually look and function.

Isn't It a Wonder?

In this project, students will work in groups to explore the Seven Wonders of the World. The Seven Wonders of the World are remarkable manmade structures—feats in engineering and planning that were built in ancient times. The project is divided into three parts:

- **Part 1:** Students will gain an understanding of the Seven Wonders of the World and why they are recognized as wonders. Each group will develop a 5-minute presentation on one of the Seven Wonders of the World.
- **Part 2:** Groups will research other well-known or not-so-well-known landmarks and nominate a new Wonder of the World. They should develop a slide presentation that discusses their new Wonder of the World, why they chose it, and why it should be considered a wonder.
- **Part 3:** Groups will create a design and/or construct a model of their own Wonder of the World. Groups will present their new wonders in a class exhibition.

Materials

- Student computer and Internet access
- Supplies for student designs/models (dependent upon what students choose to create)
- Project Outline: Isn't It a Wonder? (student copies)
- Suggested Timeline
- Handout 6.1: Researching a Wonder (student copies)
- Handout 6.2: A Modern Wonder (student copies)
- Handout 6.3: Creating a Wonder (student copies)
- Product Rubric: Isn't It a Wonder? (student copies)

Name: ______________________________ Date: ______________

PROJECT OUTLINE

Isn't It a Wonder?

Big Idea

The Wonders of the World are remarkable manmade structures—feats in engineering and planning.

Essential Question

What would a structure have to look like in order to be considered a Wonder of the World?

Deliverables

You will work in a group to explore the Seven Wonders of the World. The project is divided into three parts:

- **Part 1:** You will gain an understanding of the Seven Wonders of the World and why they are recognized as wonders. Your group will develop a 5-minute presentation on one of the Seven Wonders of the World.
- **Part 2:** Your group will research other well-known or not-so-well-known modern landmarks and nominate a new Wonder of the World. You should develop a slide presentation that discusses your new Wonder of the World, why you chose it, and why it should be considered a wonder.
- **Part 3:** Your group will create a design and/or construct a model of your own Wonder of the World. You will present your new wonder in a class exhibition.

Constraints

Modern wonders (Part 2) must still exist.

SUGGESTED TIMELINE

DAY				
1 Introduce the project. Ask students what they know about the Seven Wonders of the World. *Ask.*	**2** Divide students into seven groups to study a Wonder of the World (see Handout 6.1). *Ask.*	**3** Have groups conduct research and prepare presentations (Part 1). *Ask.*	**4** Have groups conduct research and prepare presentations (Part 1). *Ask.*	**5** Have groups present their 5-minute presentations (Part 1). *Ask.*
6 Have groups explore potential new wonders (see Handout 6.2). *Imagine.*	**7** Have groups research a new wonder (Part 2). *Imagine.*	**8** Have groups research a new wonder (Part 2). *Imagine.*	**9** Have groups research a new wonder (Part 2). *Imagine.*	**10** Have groups present their new wonders (Part 2). *Imagine.*
11 Have groups explore ideas for their own wonders (see Handout 6.3). *Imagine.*	**12** Have groups plan their own wonders (Part 3). *Plan.*	**13** Have groups design their own wonders (Part 3). *Create.*	**14** Have groups design their own wonders (Part 3). *Create/ Improve.*	**15** Have groups exhibit their new Wonders of the World.

Name: ______________________ Date: ______________

HANDOUT 6.1

Researching a Wonder

Directions: Your group is responsible for researching one of the classic Seven Wonders of the World:

- Lighthouse of Alexandria
- Great Pyramid of Giza
- Colossus of Rhodes
- Statue of Zeus at Olympia
- Hanging Gardens of Babylon
- Temple of Artemis at Ephesus
- Mausoleum at Halicarnassus

You will develop a brief 5-minute presentation about your wonder. You should include:

- a drawing or photo of what the Wonder was believed to have looked like,
- who built it and how,
- the years it is believed to have been in existence,
- what it was used for and/or its purpose,
- five interesting facts, and
- an argument for why it would have been considered a Wonder of the World.

You may use this handout to record your research. Use separate sheets of paper as needed.

Name of Wonder: ______________________

What:

Where:

When:

Name: ______________________________ Date: ________________

Handout 6.1: Researching a Wonder, *continued*

Who:

Why:

How:

Five interesting facts:

Dimension and materials the Wonder is made of:

Explanation of why you think this would be considered a Wonder of the World:

Name: ______________________________ Date: ______________

HANDOUT 6.2

A Modern Wonder

Directions: The Seven Ancient Wonders of the World are just that—ancient. Your group has been charged with updating the list to include a modern structure. Research and nominate a new Wonder of the World.

Develop a slide presentation about your new wonder that includes:

- its dimensions, what it is made of, and how it was built;
- what purpose it serves;
- several photos of the structure; and
- five reasons why it should be considered a Wonder of the World.

You may use this handout to record your research. Use separate sheets of paper as needed.

Name of Wonder: ______________________________

What:

Where:

When:

Name: ______________________________ Date: ____________________

Handout 6.2: A Modern Wonder, *continued*

Who:

Why:

How:

Dimension and materials the Wonder is made of:

Five reasons this structure should be a Wonder of the World:

Name: ______________________________ Date: ______________

HANDOUT 6.3

Creating a Wonder

Directions: You and your design team have been given the task of designing a new Wonder of the World.

Your design and/or model must:

- display the structure's actual dimensions, what it is made of, and what purpose it serves;
- identify where the structure will be located and why you chose this location;
- include several drawings; and
- list five reasons why the structure should be considered a Wonder of World.

Use this handout and/or separate sheets of paper to sketch ideas and begin planning.

Name: ______________________ Date: ______________

PRODUCT RUBRIC

Isn't It a Wonder?

	Part 1	Part 2	Part 3
Great	Presentation includes detailed facts that fulfill the requirements. Presentation includes a visual that shows in detail what the wonder looked like. Presentation provides a clear argument as to why the structure was a Wonder of the World.	Slide presentation includes detailed facts that fulfill the requirements. Slides include many visuals that show the structure in detail. Slide presentation provides a clear argument as to why the structure should be a Wonder of the World.	Design/model includes detailed facts about the structure. Design/model shows in detail the many dimensions of this structure. Design/model includes more than five reasons why the structure should be a Wonder of the World.
Good	Presentation includes facts that mostly fulfill the requirements, but more detail could be included. Presentation includes a visual that gives a general idea what the wonder looked like. Presentation provides an argument as to why the structure was a Wonder of the World, but it could be more convincing.	Slide presentation includes facts that mostly fulfill the requirements, but more detail could be included. Slides include a few visuals that give a general idea of what the structure looks like. Slide presentation provides an argument as to why the structure should be a Wonder of the World, but it could be more convincing.	Design/model includes facts that mostly fulfill the requirements, but more detail could be included. Design/model shows the many dimensions of this structure, but more detail could be included. Design/model provides five arguments for why the structure should be a Wonder of the World.

Name: ______________________ Date: ______________

Product Rubric: Isn't It a Wonder?, *continued*

	Part 1	Part 2	Part 3
Needs Improvement	Presentation does not include facts that fulfill all of the requirements. Presentation does not include a visual or does not show a correct visual. Presentation does not provide an argument as to why the structure was a Wonder of the World.	Slide presentation does not include facts that fulfill all of the requirements. Slides include few or no visuals. Slide presentation does not provide an argument as to why the structure should be a Wonder of the World.	Design/model does not include facts that fulfill all of the requirements. Design/model does not provide dimensions of the structure; viewers cannot tell what it looks like. Design/model provides fewer than five arguments for why the structure should be a Wonder of the World.

7 Record and Analyze Data

One of the most important things STEM professionals must do while conducting an experiment or research is to record the data they collect. This is because they are following the engineering design process, and if they wish to replicate their results, they need to keep track of what they did.

Recording data over time can be a valuable tool. We do this with students, recording grades and evaluations over the course of the year to determine whether the student is ready to move on to the next level. We use this data to adjust our teaching and ensure that students get what they need in the classroom, so we are constantly analyzing the data to inform our decisions. We record data in the form of memories and use it to make decisions all of the time. For example, if a person goes to a restaurant and receives bad service, he or she is probably going to be hesitant to return. If the person does go back and feels treated badly a second time, it is very unlikely this person will ever eat at this restaurant again. Businesses analyze data to predict what they need to do in order to turn a profit. They look at the history of sales and how the market is trending. They then try to predict whether the trends will continue, or they can make changes to try to increase profits.

DOI: 10.4324/9781003232520-8

The key is to organize data so that it can be understood and interpreted. Students need to be shown what organizational tools are at their disposal and then decide which ones will best display their data. The best graphic organizer to use is the one that will allow anyone to access and understand the data. That means properly labeling and having a key so that others can understand what the data are showing.

Organizing data is a good skill for students, especially gifted ones, to learn and practice. Students sometimes have grandiose notions but cannot funnel them into a form that can be shared and reflected on with others. Learning how to do this will lead to more purposeful reflection. Through reflection, the most valuable learning takes place. There is sometimes a difference between what you want students to learn and what they actually learn. And each student might have a different takeaway from a lesson or activity. It is important to create space where students can reflect upon their own learning. Sometimes students do this through portfolios in which they build a collection of their own work over the course of a semester or year. To make a portfolio meaningful, students need to analyze how or if they have grown over the course of the year. This is where that reflection takes place. Whenever students are looking at data over time, there needs to be an opportunity for them to reflect upon what was learned.

Fantasy Baseball

In this project, students will create their own fantasy baseball teams and explore how baseball is a game involving statistics, percentages, decimals, and other math concepts. Students will determine the total batting average, on-base percentage, number of runs batted in (RBIs), number of home runs scored, and number of runs scored for their teams over the course of 3 consecutive weeks.

Materials

- Student computer and Internet access
- Project Outline: Fantasy Baseball
- Suggested Timeline
- Lesson: Determining Baseball Statistics

- Handout 7.1: Building Your Team (student copies)
- Handout 7.2: Recording Your Team's Stats (several copies per student in order to record data over the course of the project)
- Handout 7.3: Averaging Your Team's Stats (student copies)

Name: ______________________________ Date: ______________

PROJECT OUTLINE

Fantasy Baseball

Big Idea

Baseball involves many mathematical concepts.

Essential Question

How do you predict how a baseball player is going to perform over the course of 3 weeks?

Deliverables

You will create your own fantasy baseball team and explore how baseball is a game involving statistics, percentages, decimals, and other math concepts. You will determine the total batting average, on-base percentage, number of runs batted in (RBIs), number of home runs scored, and number of runs scored for your team over the course of 3 consecutive weeks.

Constraints

You must:

- complete this project during baseball season,
- record data for 3 consecutive weeks (or 21 days),
- keep track of your team's statistics, and
- only count statistics from your starting lineup (although you can move players from the bench to the starting lineup).

SUGGESTED TIMELINE

DAY				
1 Introduce the project and conduct Lesson: Determining Baseball Statistics. *Ask.*	**2** Have students begin researching players they would like to select (see Handout 7.1). *Imagine.*	**3** Have students select their team rosters. *Plan.*	**4** Students must record data from the day before (see Handout 7.2). *Create.*	**5** Students must record data from the day before. *Create.*
6 Students must record data from the weekend. *Create.*	**7** Students must record data from the day before. *Create.*	**8** Students must record data from the day before. *Create.*	**9** Students must record data from the day before. *Create.*	**10** Students must record data from the day before. *Create.*
11 Students must record data from the weekend. *Create.*	**12** Students must record data from the day before. *Create.*	**13** Students must record data from the day before. *Create.*	**14** Students must record data from the day before. *Create.*	**15** Students must record data from the day before. *Create.*
6 Students must record data from the weekend. *Create.*	**17** Students must record data from the day before. *Create.*	**18** Students must record data from the day before. *Create.*	**19** Students must determine their teams averages/totals (see Handout 7.3). *Improve.*	**20** Have students compare their results to others in the class, determining who had the best fantasy team.

LESSON

Determining Baseball Statistics

1. Ask students what they know about baseball statistics. Explain that stats are how to keep track of a player's performance throughout a season or throughout his career. In this project, students will explore five different stats: batting average, on-base percentage, home runs, runs batted in (RBIs), and runs scored.
2. Tell students that a batting average is calculated by dividing the number of hits a player has by the number of at bats (i.e., time at bat). For example, if a player has 18 hits in 54 at bats, his batting average is .333 (18 ÷ 54 = .333).
3. On-base percentage is the number of hits + walks + hit by pitch divided by a player's number of plate appearances. For example, if a player has 18 hits + 7 walks + 1 hit and 64 plate appearances, his on-base percentage is .406 (18 + 7 + 1 = 26 ÷ 64 = .406).
4. A home run is counted each time a player is able to circle all four bases and touch home plate in one at bat. The most common home run is when a player hits the ball over the fence, but there are rare inside-the-park homeruns when the ball is hit and gets away from the fielder, and the batter is able to make it around all the bases quickly. To calculate number of home runs, simply add them together.
5. Runs batted in are when a batter makes a play that allows a run to be scored. To calculate runs batted in, simply add them together.
6. Runs scored are the number of times a player crosses home plate and scores a run for his team. To calculate runs, simply add them together.
7. Explain to students that, beyond calculating these statistics, there are certain benchmarks to look out for. For example, a .300 batting average is considered to be pretty good. Over the course of a season, 30 or more home runs is above average. For RBIs and runs scored, the benchmark is more than 100. An on-base percentage above .400 is really good.
8. In order to build their fantasy teams, students will want to select players who, in the course of the 3 weeks, will likely perform well in these categories.

Name: ______________________________ Date: ______________

HANDOUT 7.1

Building Your Team

Directions: In order to build your fantasy team, you need to find out which players play which position and learn more about their career stats as well as their stats for the current year.

The Major League Baseball site (https://www.mlb.com) is a great place to start; however, you are welcome to seek other sources. You can specifically go to http://mlb.mlb.com/mlb/players/?tcid=nav_mlb_players to search for players by position.

As you seek team members to fill your nine available positions, there are a few things to consider about each player:

- Does this player play this position a majority of the time?
- Is this an everyday player?
- Is this player injured?
- Does this player typically perform well in these stats?

My Players

Position	Player	Team
First Base		
Second Base		
Third Base		
Shortstop		
Catcher		
Left Field		
Center Field		
Right Field		
Designated Hitter		

Name: ______________________________ Date: ______________

HANDOUT 7.2

Recording Your Team's Stats

Directions: Each day over the next 3 weeks, you will gather information for your team's stats. You can check your local paper or visit the Major League Baseball site at http://mlb.mlb.com/stats/sortable. You can click on the "Yesterday" tab at the top in order to look for your players and how they did. You can also search by team if you like.

Day: ______________________________

Position	Hits	At Bats	Walks/Hit by Pitch	Plate Appearances	Home Runs	RBIs	Runs
First Base							
Second Base							
Third Base							
Shortstop							
Catcher							
Left Field							
Center Field							
Right Field							
Designated Hitter							
Totals							

Name: ____________________ Date: ____________

HANDOUT 7.3

Averaging Your Team's Stats

Directions: Tabulate your 3 weeks of statistics to average and total your team's stats. For example, if your team had 29 hits over the course of the 3 weeks, you would divide this by the total number of at bats your players had, which is 92. This would give you a team average of .315. Calculate your team's averages and totals for each stat.

Position	Total # of Hits	Total # of At Bats	Total # of Walks/Hit by Pitch	Total # of Plate Appearances	Total # of Home Runs	Total # of RBIs	Total # of Runs
First Base							
Second Base							
Third Base							
Shortstop							
Catcher							
Left Field							
Center Field							
Right Field							
Designated Hitter							
Totals							

Project 7: Record and Analyze Data

Name: ______________________________ Date: ______________

Handout 7.3: Averaging Your Team's Stats, *continued*

	Team Totals
Batting Average	
On-Base Percentage	
Home Runs	
RBIs	
Runs Scored	

8 Investigate Change Over Time and Patterns

One of the most valuable things you can teach students is that history repeats itself. Consider World War I and World War II, the assassinations of Abraham Lincoln and John F. Kennedy, and the fall of the Greek and Roman Empires. Students may wonder, "How do you avoid history repeating itself?" The answer is: by learning from it. By studying patterns and trends, students can make educated predictions. Consider global warming and climate change. Scientists have noticed a trend that the world is getting warmer, as pollution destroys the ozone a little bit every year. As a result of this pattern, humans are working to combat climate change by cutting down on emissions that cause this deterioration.

Patterns are evident in the advancement of technology, with a new iPhone coming out each year, computers getting smaller and smarter, and self-driving cars becoming more commonplace. It is the study of these advances in technology that leads to further advancements. We are constantly trying to make things better. It is human nature. By studying changes over time, we are able to determine what we do not need anymore, what we need to continue to do, and what we need to add to improve something

DOI: 10.4324/9781003232520-9

In the classroom, we do not have the luxury of studying something firsthand over a long period of time. But we can run an experiment for a few weeks, chart observations over a limited period of time, run a brief investigation of what may happen, and study the past to determine how elements change over time.

Egg Drop Challenge

In this project, students will work in groups to utilize their engineering skills to create a structure that will allow them to safely drop an egg from a distance of at least 10 feet (or higher depending on teacher discretion and/or what is available to the class) without breaking the egg. The egg drop vessel can only be made from select types of materials. Students may only choose five of the following materials to create their structures: 5 plastic straws, 5 craft sticks, a 16-inch strip of tape, 5 sheets of paper, a small bottle of glue, 1 plastic bag, an 8.5 x 11-inch piece of cardboard, 1 sock, or 1 balloon.

Note. Share with students some videos of egg drop challenges, such as "Egg Drop Challenge! Try Not to Break It" (available at https://www.youtube.com/watch?v=vMDtiYhoymc) or "Egg Drop Project" (available at https://www.youtube.com/watch?v=vTQZKo_OxF4).

At the end of the project, ask groups to debrief and discuss how much their vessels changed throughout each stage (design, first model, improved model, testing model).

Materials

- Supplies for students' egg-drop vessels (plastic straws, craft sticks, tape, paper, glue, plastic bags, cardboard, socks, balloons)
- Project Outline: Egg Drop Challenge (student copies)
- Suggested Timeline
- Handout 8.1: Egg Drop Design (student copies)
- Handout 8.2: Egg Drop Testing (student copies)
- Product Rubric: Egg Drop Challenge (student copies)

Name: ______________________________ Date: ______________

PROJECT OUTLINE

Egg Drop Challenge

Big Idea

The engineering design process allows you to plan, test, and refine an idea.

Essential Question

How can you use engineering practices to safely drop an egg?

Deliverables

Working with a group, you will utilize your engineering skills to create a structure that will allow you to safely drop an egg from a distance of at least 10 feet without breaking the egg. The egg-drop vessel can only be made from select types of materials.

Constraints

You may only choose five of the following materials to create your structure:

- 5 plastic straws,
- 5 craft sticks,
- a 16-inch strip of tape,
- 5 sheets of paper,
- a small bottle of glue,
- 1 plastic bag,
- an 8.5 x 11-inch piece of cardboard
- 1 sock, or
- 1 balloon.

SUGGESTED TIMELINE

DAY 1	2	3	4	5
Introduce the project and divide students into groups. *Ask.*	Have teams decide on their materials (see Handout 8.1). *Imagine.*	Have teams decide on their materials. *Imagine.*	Have teams plan their structures. *Plan.*	Have teams begin building their structures. *Create.*
6 Have teams build their structures. *Create.*	**7** Have teams complete their structures. *Create.*	**8** Have groups test their structures (see Handout 8.2). *Improve.*	**9** Have teams revise their structures. *Improve.*	**10** Conduct a final egg drop challenge. Have teams debrief.

Name: ______________________________ Date: ______________

HANDOUT 8.1

Egg Drop Design

Directions: In order to begin constructing your egg drop vessel, you must first select your materials and then begin to develop an initial design.

Egg Drop Material Choices

1. ______________________________
2. ______________________________
3. ______________________________
4. ______________________________
5. ______________________________

Hints on Creating a Design

- Start with a rough draft.
- Use proper drawing tools (e.g., ruler, compass) for the final version.
- Show how you will incorporate all of the materials.
- Label the different parts of the design, writing clearly in print.
- Make the design recognizable enough for others to understand.

Name: ______________________________ Date: ______________

HANDOUT 8.2

Egg Drop Testing

Directions: Using a golf ball, test your vessel, standing on a chair to drop it. Look for patterns and trends that are successful and ones that are not. You want to improve your device in order to ensure success. What do you learn each time you drop your vessel?

Discuss the following questions with your team after each drop test.

1. Was there a hard impact?
2. Would the vessel survive from a higher drop?
3. What is not needed that can be removed from the vessel?
4. Is there anything that needs to be added using the materials you have available?
5. Are there any other changes to the vessel that need to be made?
6. Are there any materials you wish you had chosen but did not?

Name: ______________________ Date: ____________

PRODUCT RUBRIC

Egg Drop Challenge

	Design	Model
Great	Design is detailed and easy to understand. Design is clearly laid out; parts, dimensions, and materials are labeled. Design looks professional; it looks like a final draft.	Team is able to secure the egg in the vessel with ease. Team uses the five materials in a creative way, adding practical use to the vessel rather than just for show. Team can explain how it improved the model from the design phase and why it made these changes.
Good	Design is easy to understand for the most part and includes appropriate detail. Design is clearly laid out for the most part; most parts, dimensions, and materials are labeled. Design looks well put together; it looks like a final draft, but not quite professional.	Team is able to secure the egg in the vessel, but it is a little complicated. Team uses the five materials, but not always practically; some are used for show. Team can explain how it improved the model from the design phase, but it is not clear why the team made these changes.
Needs Improvement	Design is not easy to understand; it is not clear what the vessel looks like. Parts, materials, and dimensions are not labeled. Design looks unprofessional; it looks like a first draft.	Team has great difficulty securing the egg in the vessel. Team does not use all of the five materials. Team cannot explain how it improved the model or why it made changes.

9 Use Computer Models or Simulations

As technology becomes more and more prevalent in education, so, too, does the issue of using it properly. Technology, like any tool, is only effective if it improves learning. There are several ways to use technology to enhance the learning of students, but one that is especially effective is the use of computer models, which allow students to ask "What if . . . ?" What if this happened instead of that, what if this had never happened, or what if we did it differently? Computer models allow students to try their solution in different ways. They can make three or four attempts at something, changing something major or just making minor tweaks, leading them closer and closer to a functional solution. Computer models allow students to fail with a safety net in place. If a student were making a model out of craft sticks only to find out halfway through that he made a mistake in his foundation, he would have to throw the entire thing out and start with new materials.

The computer program *Sim City* is an excellent example. You can build entire cities, including infrastructure, buildings, and other items crucial to the success of a city. The program alerts you if your city is not performing like it should. If you do not string enough electricity throughout the city, there are homes and businesses that will be without electricity. This makes

DOI: 10.4324/9781003232520-10

it difficult for them to be successful. If you put the fire department on one side of town only to have a fire break out on the complete opposite side, by the time the fire truck gets to its destination, the building will have burned down. If the town becomes too unhappy, you start to lose residents, and when that happens, you lose money needed to keep building. If you have enough problems with the city, you can simply hit the destruct button and bring the whole thing to the ground and start all over again.

How many times were you playing a video game, such as *Donkey Kong*, only to either be hit by a barrel, caught on fire by a fireball, or have the bouncy thing land on your head? When failure happened, what did you do? You put another quarter in the slot and tried again. You would try and fail for hours on end. Nowadays with Microsoft Xbox, Nintendo Switch, and Sony PlayStation, simply pushing a button allows you to try again. This process is all about learning—learning what you did wrong, learning what not to do, learning what works. This is the sort of resilience we should bring into the classroom.

Computer simulations make problem solving more authentic because they put students in the shoes of the person or people experiencing the problem, and they are also excellent examples of learning from failure. Using computer simulations and models to teach students that failure is okay encourages students to take risks. Taking a risk is where the most learning takes place. This is the power technology can have in the classroom.

What Are the Consequences?

In this project, students will construct a computer simulation or animation in which they change a significant event in time. Students must show five consequences of their selected event once history has been altered and how the consequences differ from the outcomes of the original event. The simulation should allow someone observing it to see how the change in history led to these effects. The effects should be brought to life—not just stated.

Students may use a program like Scratch or a program of their choosing to develop their simulation or animation. If students have difficulty finding a program, students could even create their project with PowerPoint or Google Slides.

Materials

- Project Outline: What Are the Consequences? (student copies)
- Suggested Timeline
- Lesson: Cause and Effect
- Handout 9.1: Changing History (student copies)
- Product Rubric: What Are the Consequences? (student copies)

Name: ______________________ Date: ______________

PROJECT OUTLINE

What Are the Consequences?

Big Idea

Cause and effect are important forces in history, as well as STEM fields.

Essential Question

How might the world change if a significant event in history went differently?

Deliverables

You will construct a computer simulation or animation in which you change a significant event in history. You must show five consequences of the event once history has been altered and how the consequences differ from outcomes of the original event. The simulation should allow someone participating in it to see how the change in history led to these effects. The effects should be brought to life—not just stated.

Constraints

You must:

- develop a computer simulation or animation,
- somehow change history, and
- show five well-researched potential consequences in detail.

SUGGESTED TIMELINE

DAY				
1 Introduce the project and conduct Lesson: Cause and Effect. *Ask/ Imagine.*	**2** Have students research and consider important events in history. *Plan.*	**3** Have students choose important events to change. *Plan.*	**4** Have students research and develop consequences. *Plan.*	**5** Have students research and develop consequences. *Plan.*
6 Have students research and develop consequences. *Plan.*	**7** Have students research and develop consequences. *Plan.*	**8** Have students research and develop consequences. *Plan.*	**9** Have students begin creating their simulations. *Create.*	**10** Have students create their simulations. *Create.*
11 Have students create their simulations. *Create.*	**12** Have students create their simulations. *Create.*	**13** Have students complete their simulations. *Create.*	**14** Have students peer review each other's simulations. *Improve.*	**15** Have students view each other's simulations.

LESSON

Cause and Effect

1. Explain that cause and effect are constantly in play. Ask students: *You have a math test tomorrow, but you've also been invited to play soccer at a friend's house tonight. Do you study for the test, or do you go play soccer at your friend's house?*
2. Ask: *If you choose to study for the test, what might happen?* (You may get a good grade, may feel like you learned something, or might be able to help a friend who didn't study, or you may do poorly anyway.)
3. Ask: *If you go play soccer, what might happen?* (You might do poorly on the test, be tired and sleep through your alarm tomorrow, or hurt your ankle and be unable to get to school, or you may still be able to achieve a good grade.)
4. Explain that this one decision has many possible effects, but most of the effects are not likely to affect someone for that long. Other causes can have effects that last for thousands or even millions of years.
5. Ask: *What if fire was never discovered?* Guide students to consider how furnaces might not exist, stoves might not exist, blacksmiths might not have been able to craft tools in the Middle Ages, and humanity might not have survived.
6. Ask: *What if the American Revolution ended differently?* Elicit responses. Students may consider that the United States would not have become a democracy, Great Britain would be the largest empire in the world, there might be a lot more tea, Spain and France might have claimed more of the United States, monuments to American Revolution heroes would not exist, etc.
7. Emphasize that all of these choices can be justified with facts and examples. For example, the United States might not have become a democracy because the British were part of a monarchy during the American Revolution. Other countries, too, like France, might not have become democratic.
8. An effect such as "aliens would have invaded the planet" would likely not have resulted from winning or losing the American Revolution.

Name: ____________________ Date: ____________

HANDOUT 9.1

Changing History

Directions: Choose an important event in history. You may want to do some initial research before selecting your event. Some things you might consider when choosing this event include:

- How much do you know about the event?
- Are there a lot of long-term effects that might change if the event went differently?
- How much is known about the cause (e.g., we don't know much about who invented the first wheel)?
- Is the event something you are interested in exploring?

Historical Event: ____________________

New Event: ____________________

Now that you have your event chosen, imagine five consequences of this event occurring differently. What happens when you change history? These effects should be justified with research or facts that support your arguments.

Consequence 1: ____________________

Cause	**The Effects**	**Justification** *(Why This Consequence Occurs)*

Name: ______________________________ Date: ______________

Handout 9.1: Changing History, *continued*

Consequence 2: ______________________________

Cause	The Effects	**Justification** *(Why This Consequence Occurs)*

Consequence 3: ______________________________

Cause	The Effects	**Justification** *(Why This Consequence Occurs)*

Name: ______________________________ Date: ______________

Handout 9.1: Changing History, *continued*

Consequence 4: ______________________________

Cause	The Effects	**Justification** *(Why This Consequence Occurs)*

Consequence 5: ______________________________

Cause	The Effects	**Justification** *(Why This Consequence Occurs)*

Name: ______________________ Date: ______________

PRODUCT RUBRIC

What Are the Consequences?

Overall	Simulation/ Animation	Content	Consequences
Great	Simulation/ animation runs smoothly; the five consequences of the change in history are clearly and effectively described. The computer animation is creative and clever; many details are included.	There are many facts used to justify the different consequences. The chosen event would have a significant impact on history. Information used comes from a reliable source.	More than five consequences are included. The effects range from short-term to long-range, providing a complete picture of the potential consequences. Effects are very logical.
Good	Simulation/ animation runs smoothly; the five consequences of the change in history are described. The computer animation is creative, but more details could be included.	There are some facts used to justify the different consequences. The chosen event would have an impact on history but not necessarily a significant one. Most of the information used seems to come from a reliable source.	Five consequences are included. The effects are either mostly short-term or long-range, making for an inconsistent picture. Effects are mostly logical, but not all are justified.
Needs Improvement	Simulation/animation does not run smoothly; the five consequences of the change in history are not described. The computer animation is not creative or detailed.	Very few facts are used to justify the different consequences. The chosen event would not have much impact on history. Most of the information used seems to come from questionable sources.	Fewer than five effects are included. The effects are either all short-term or long-range, making for an unclear picture. Effects seem illogical.

10 Construct and Explain Systems

Systems can be quite complicated. Take our political system, for example. A basic understanding of it is that there are three branches of government, each watching the others to make sure there is no abuse of power. In practice, we know it is far more complex than this. Because many systems are so complex, from ecosystems to the Earth's climate to the solar system, having the ability to analyze complicated systems and describe them concisely and accurately is a valuable skill.

We start small with students, asking them to understand ecosystems, how the economy works, systems of equations, or what system to use in order to write a clear essay. We ask students to explain systems, or write them, or to be able to explain them visually. By being able to understand a system, students are able to see both the big picture as well as the little details. Usually when people fail at systems, it is because they either do not see the big picture or do not understand how the details are put together to create it. Understanding systems is a valuable skill for students to possess indeed.

DOI: 10.4324/9781003232520-11

The Game of Economics

In this project, students will work in groups to develop a game that teaches economic and math concepts, and requires players to use an economic concept to win the game.

Materials

- A variety of economic board games for students to play (Monopoly, The Game of Life, Pay Day, Careers, Modern Art, Who Wants to Be a Millionaire?, Ticket to Ride, Acquire, Settlers of Catan, Wealth of Nations, etc.)
- Student computer and Internet access
- Supplies for student games (dependent upon students' plans)
- Project Outline: The Game of Economics (student copies)
- Suggested Timeline
- Lesson: Economics in Games
- Lesson: Writing Clear Instructions
- Handout 10.1: Planning Your Game (student copies)
- Product Rubric: The Game of Economics (student copies)

Name: ______________________________ Date: ______________

PROJECT OUTLINE

The Game of Economics

Big Idea

Games can be valuable teaching tools.

Essential Question

How can you demonstrate an economic concept through a board game?

Deliverables

You will work in a group to develop a game that teaches economic and math concepts, and requires players to use an economic concept to win the game.

Constraints

You must include:

- a title for the game,
- all game pieces and/or a board (if needed),
- an explanation of how math is used in the game,
- a set of clear instructions for how to play and win, and
- a container for the game.

SUGGESTED TIMELINE

DAY				
1 Introduce the project and conduct Lesson: Economics in Games. *Ask.*	**2** Have students play a variety of economic board games. *Ask.*	**3** Divide students into groups and assign groups an economic concept to research. *Imagine.*	**4** Have groups research their economic concepts. *Imagine.*	**5** Have groups brainstorm how to implement their games. *Imagine.*
6 Have groups plan their board games. *Plan.*	**6** Have groups plan their board games. *Plan.*	**8** Have groups plan their board games. *Plan.*	**9** Have groups begin to make their board games. *Create.*	**10** Have groups make their board games. *Create.*
11 Have groups make their board games. *Create.*	**11** Have groups make their board games. *Create.*	**13** Have groups complete their board games. *Create.*	**14** Have groups play their own board games and make improvements. *Improve.*	**15** Have students play other students' board games.

LESSON

Economics in Games

1. Ask students: *Have you ever played Monopoly? How is it played?* Elicit student responses. Explain that Monopoly is a game where the goal is to buy properties and develop them with houses and hotels. Players who land on a space owned by another player are charged rent, so the player who owns the property makes money to buy more property. Eventually the person who bankrupts all of their opponents and/or has the most or all of the money wins.
2. Ask: *How is math used in Monopoly?* Guide students to understand that there are several math concepts utilized in Monopoly, such as in:
   - the exchange of money,
   - determining percentages of salary when taxed,
   - using statistics to determine which spaces are most often landed on, and
   - the probability of a role of the dice.

3. Tell students that there are several economic concepts employed in the game:
   - **Supply and demand:** Some properties are more highly coveted than others, especially if someone is trying to make a monopoly. When players negotiate a trade, someone with a high demand and low supply can sell his property for more money.
   - **Competition:** Players compete to buy the properties and accumulate the most money. It is a fair game, not an equal game.
   - **Monopolies:** By collecting all of the properties in a certain strand, players are able to charge more for them and increase the likelihood that someone will land on one of them because they take up so much space.
   - **Scarcity:** As more and more properties are bought up, resources become less available or scarce.
   - **Entrepreneurship:** Players build their own businesses, buying houses and hotels to develop their real estate and charging other players rent.

4. There is a variety of other games that teach economics concepts, such as The Game of Life, Pay Day, Careers, Who Wants to Be a Millionaire?, Modern Art, or Ticket to Ride. There are also some more complex games, such as Acquire, Puerto Rico, Agricola, Settlers of Catan, Power Grid, and Wealth of Nations. Tell students that over the next two days they will explore some of these games.

5. (Optional) As a class, play The Trading Game, where students simulate trade between countries. Resources for the game are available at https://myedexpert.com/item/the-trading-game.
6. After students play several games, debrief. Discuss which economic concepts appear in each game.

LESSON

Writing Clear Instructions

1. Ask students: *When you play a board game for the first time, how do you learn to play it?* Guide students to understand that there is always a set of directions that explain how to play the game. The directions always need to be clear so that players understand what to do.
2. Ask: *Have you ever played Mancala? What if you were only provided with the following instructions for how to play?*

> The game is over when a player has no more stones on his or her side of the board. The winner is the player with the greatest total of stones in his or her mancala and any remaining stones on his or her side of the board.

3. Ask: *What is wrong with these directions?* Elicit responses. Students many note that many instructions are missing: The instructions do not say how many stones start on which side of the board, how players get rid of the stones from their side, how to set up the board, how many players can play, or what the mancala is.
4. Have students study the instructions from the board games that they played during the previous lesson. Ask: *What are some qualities of effective instructions?* Students may notice that well-written instructions break the directions into categories (e.g., the materials to play the game, the setup of the board, the object of the game, how to play, and how to win). Good instructions also make the steps to play easy to follow and in chronological order, usually by numbering them. Illustrations are also sometimes provided. Explain that students need to ensure that their games have clear instructions so that new players know what to do.

Name: ______________________________ Date: ______________

HANDOUT 10.1

Planning Your Game

Directions: In order to create your board game, your group will be assigned 1–2 of the following 10 economic concepts:

1. Productive resources
2. Entrepreneurship
3. Trade-offs
4. Specialization
5. Absolute advantage
6. Comparative advantage
7. Economic interdependence
8. Supply and demand
9. Scarcity
10. Private/public sector

Some things to consider when making your game:

- Your game does not have to be a board game. It can utilize cards, be an active game, or even be a computer game.
- The simpler you make your game, the better.
- Your game needs to have clear directions so players can easily learn how to play. You will not be able to explain verbally to people how to play.
- Everyone in your group needs to contribute. You can divide up tasks and accomplish more than everyone working on the same thing together.
- You need to determine how to demonstrate the math involved with your economic concept.
- You can model your game after an already existing game, but it does need to be original.
- You will need to start by researching your economic concept(s) and making sure all of your group members have a clear understanding of not only what the concept is but also how it could be demonstrated.

Name: ______________________ Date: ______________

PRODUCT RUBRIC

The Game of Economics

Overall	Game	Economic Concept	Directions
Great	Game looks professional; the proper pieces and/or cards are included for players. Design of the game is very creative and ties into the economic concept well. Game has a container that looks like a real game and holds all of the materials needed for it.	Required economic concept(s) is obviously in use during game play, allowing players to gain understanding of the concept(s). Game developers clearly understand the economic concept(s). Economic concept(s) is central to how players win the game and is in use throughout the game.	Directions are very clear and well organized; step-by-step instructions of how to play and win the game are provided. Directions are typed or written neatly; they are easy to see and read.
Good	Game looks well put together; almost all of the proper pieces and/or cards are included for players. Design of the game is creative and ties into the economic concept, but more details could be provided. Game has a container that holds all of the materials, but it could look more professional.	Required economic concept(s) is in use during game play, allowing players to gain a general understanding of the concept(s). Game developers understand the economic concept(s), but they could have a deeper understanding. Economic concept(s) is part of how players win the game, but it could have been a bigger focus.	Directions are clear, but they could be better organized or include more detail. Directions are typed or written; they are easy to see and read for the most part.

Project 10: Construct and Explain Systems

Name: ______________________________ Date: ______________

Product Rubric: The Game of Economics, *continued*

Overall	Game	Economic Concept	Directions
Needs Improvement	Game does not look well put together; the proper pieces and/or cards are not included for players. Design of the game is not creative and/or does not tie into the economic concept. Game does not have a container and/or the container does not hold all of the materials.	Required economic concept(s) is rarely in use during game play; players do not grasp the concept(s). Game developers have misunderstood the economic concept(s). Economic concept(s) is not part of how players win the game.	Directions are unclear or completely lack detail. Directions are not typed or written; or they are sloppy and are not easy to see and read.

DEVELOP YOUR OWN STEM PROJECTS

You can develop your own projects through the cycle depicted in Figure 5.

Define a Problem

Defining a problem can be handled in many different ways depending on the needs of the class and curriculum. One option is to base it on standards. Consider the Common Core Standards in math and language arts and the Next Generation Science Standards (NGSS). You could choose one of these as the basis of your problem. For example, here is a fifth-grade science standard from the NGSS:

> 5 ESS1-1 Support an argument that the apparent brightness of the sun and stars is due to their relative distances from the Earth.

One could easily construct a project from this problem, having students create a model that shows the relative distances of the sun and nearby stars. Students could even create a demonstration using flashlights that show the varying brightness of these objects as a result of distance.

You could also start with a national STEM learning goal, such as those that make up the structure of this book. Alternatively, you could consider 21st-century skills, such as collaboration and teamwork, creativity and imagination, critical thinking, problem solving, oral and written communication skills, social responsibility and citizenship, technology literacy, and initiative. You could choose from one or more of these areas and

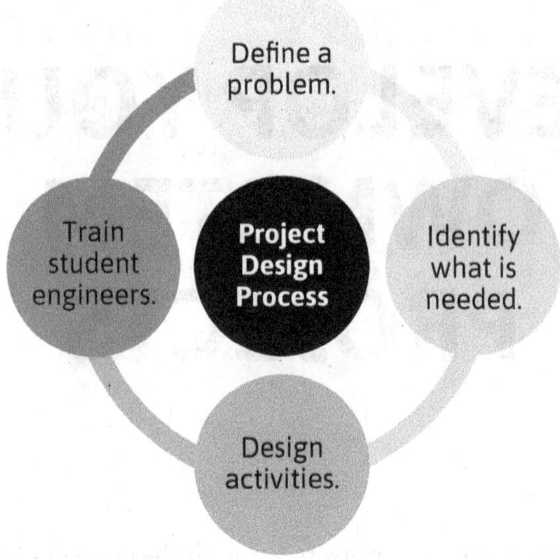

FIGURE 5. Project design process.

develop a project. For example, if you wanted to focus on oral communication, you would have to design your project so that the final product required students to give an oral presentation to an authentic audience.

Yet another way to define a project is by exploring an authentic, real-world problem. Say there is an opioid problem in your school district, or your school is trying to figure out an effective way to run its recycling program. You could take either of these real-world situations and ask students to develop solutions.

Identify What Is Needed

The best way to figure out what is needed for a project is to start at the end. What do you want students to ideally turn in at the end of the project? What would this product look like or involve? Everything stems from this product, including the skills needed to accomplish it and the lessons you will need to teach in order for students to understand what they are doing. You want to have a general idea of what this product is going to look like, but you should not be so detailed that there is little student choice. As much as possible, you should provide students with choices in their products. This is where creativity comes into play as well as student empowerment. Providing students with choice engages them in the learning and will probably lead to a better quality product.

Once you have decided what the product is going to be, you can create the rubric that is going to evaluate it. This is where you set the performance criteria. This should be based on whatever way you chose to define the problem. For instance, if you are focusing on a very specific content standard, this should be reflected in the rubric. However, if you instead decided to focus on a 21st-century skill, the criteria for how to evaluate it need to be laid out in the rubric.

Design Activities

Once the product is put into place, you can backward build the rest of the project. I actually like to use a calendar like you see at the beginning of the projects in this book, putting the final product at the end and then building outward from there. For instance, if the project we were having students work on had a final product of a portfolio, I would have to consider what skills students need to employ and what information they need to find in order to complete the project.

If I were doing a project where students had to create a new mousetrap, one that did not harm the mouse, I would start with the completed mousetrap and then build backward from there. It might look like Figure 6.

This would be plotted out step by step until I reached the beginning of the project when it is being introduced to students. Then, I would go back and determine how much time I would need for each of step and plug the steps into a calendar. The final step is to reverse the order and make sure the project is following the engineering design process (see Figure 7).

Train Student Engineers

Now that you have the project figured out and the product determined, the most challenging part occurs. This is where the teacher has to train his or her student engineers. This means making sure that students have a firm understanding of how the engineering design process works because it will be the backbone of every STEM project.

Part of this training may include how to work effectively in groups, because STEM projects often require students to have partners or multiple team members. No matter students' age, it would be wrong to assume that

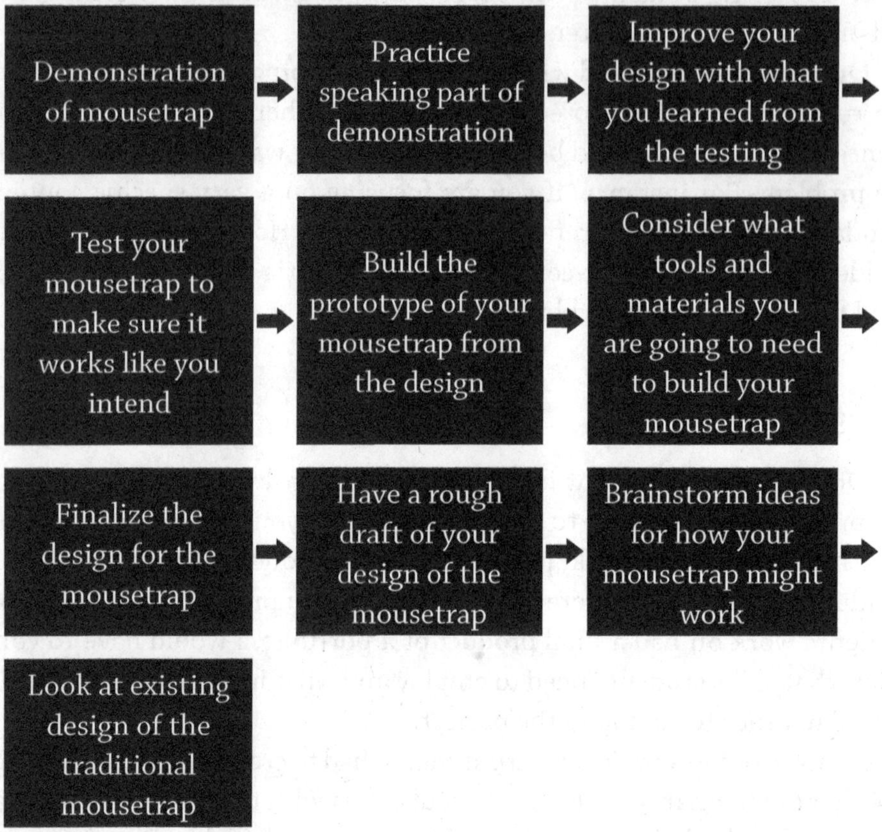

FIGURE 6. Sample of backward building.

they already know how to work with others successfully in the group setting. You will want to make sure to take some time to practice team-working skills and have guidelines for proper group behavior and expectations. You also need to determine ways to evaluate students not just on the overall product produced by the group, but also on what each student's contribution to that product was. If two students turn in the same work, but one contributed 90% of the work, it is not fair to give both an equal grade.

The role of the teacher shifts from being in front of the room, to acting as a coach from the side. It involves conversations with students and keen observation skills to determine when a group or student needs some help, and when you need to let them figure something out for themselves. Part of this is determining how to best use time and space—time in the form of opportunities for students to test and improve their results, and space in the form of learning without interference of the teacher. The best learning

DAY **1** Introduce the project; review the design of the original mousetrap. *Ask.*	**2** Introduce students to the engineering design process. Allow them to begin brainstorming ideas. *Ask/Imagine.*	**3** Students begin to design their new mousetrap, conducting research to make sure it does not already exist. *Imagine/Plan.*	**4** Students finish designing their new mousetrap. *Plan.*	**5** Students create a list of materials needed to make the model of the mousetrap. *Plan.*
6 Students construct model of mousetrap. *Create.*	**7** Students construct model of mousetrap. *Create.*	**8** Students test mousetrap and make any improvements they think are needed. *Improve.*	**9** Students finish construction of model of mousetrap and test to make sure it works as intended. *Improve.*	**10** Students practice the speaking part of their demonstrations. *Improve.*
11 Students demonstrate their mousetraps.				

FIGURE 7. Sample project calendar. Adapted from *10 Performance-Based Projects for the Science Classroom* (p. 99), by T. Stanley, 2017, New York, NY: Taylor & Francis. Copyright 2017 by Taylor & Francis. Adapted with permission.

is discovery learning, which, as a teacher, means sometimes figuring out how to get out of students' way.

Your role is to manage the project, not determine its path. You will need to figure out what skills students might need to have before they can be successful. For instance, if the project calls for students to conduct interviews, do they have the knowledge of how to do these, or are there tips and guidelines you can point them to in order to make their chances for meaningful success that much greater? Keep in mind that most of the heavy lifting should be done by the students.

REFERENCES

Advancement Courses. (2015). *The engineering design process: The 4 key steps to STEM teaching and learning* [Web log post]. Retrieved from https://www.advancementcourses.com/blog/the-engineering-design-process-the-4-key-steps-to-stem-teaching-and-learning

Boaler, J. (2002). Learning from teaching: Exploring the relationship between reform curriculum and equity. *Journal for Research in Mathematics Education, 33,* 239–258.

Buck Institute for Education. (n.d.). *Why PBL?* Retrieved from https://www.bie.org/about/why_pbl

Condliffe, B. (2017). *Project-based learning: A literature review* [Working paper]. New York, NY: MDRC.

Creative Learning Exchange. (2016). *Using system dynamics and systems thinking (SD/ST) tools and learning strategies to build science, technology, engineering, and math excellence.* Retrieved from http://www.clexchange.org/curriculum/standards/stem.asp

Deitering, S. (2016). *Is project based learning a more effective way of teaching than traditional teaching?* (Master's thesis, Northwestern College, Orange City, IA). Retrieved from https://nwcommons.nwciowa.edu/education_masters/12

Dintersmith, T., & Whiteley, G. (2015). *Most likely to succeed* [Motion picture]. United States: One Potato Productions.

Engineering is Elementary. (2018). *The engineering design process.* Retrieved from https://www.eie.org/overview/engineering-design-process

Graduate Management Admission Council. (2018). *Employers seek communication skills in new hires*. Retrieved from https://www.mba.com/mbas-and-business-masters/articles/your-career-path/employers-seek-communications-skills

Guinness World Records. (n.d.). *Farthest distance to fire a pumpkin*. Retrieved from http://www.guinnessworldrecords.com/world-records/farthest-distance-to-fire-a-pumpkin

International Technology and Engineering Educators Association. (2016). *About*. Retrieved from https://www.iteea.org/About.aspx

Mathison, S., & Feeman, M. (1997). *The logic of interdisciplinary studies*. Presented at the Annual Meeting of the American Educational Research Association, Chicago, IL.

Menzies, V., Hewitt, C., Kokotsaki, D., Collyer, C., & Wiggins, A. (2016). *Project-based learning: Evaluation report and executive summary*. London, England: Education Endowment Foundation.

Partnership for 21st Century Skills. (2016). *P21 framework definitions*. Washington, DC: Author.

Scholastic. (n.d.). *Building abstract thinking through math*. Retrieved from https://www.scholastic.com/teachers/articles/teaching-content/building-abstract-thinking-through-math

Stanley, T. (2015). *Creating life-long learners: Using project-based management to teach 21st century skills*. Thousand Oaks, CA: Corwin.

Stanley, T. (2017). *10 performance-based projects for the science classroom*. Waco, TX: Prufrock Press.

Stanley, T. (2018). *When smart kids underachieve in school: Practical solutions for teachers*. Waco, TX: Prufrock Press.

Thomas, J. W. (2000). *A review of research on project-based learning*. San Rafael, CA: Autodesk Foundation.

Waters, M. (1992). Auction: First lines. In R. Behn & C. Twichell, *The practice of poetry: Writing exercise from poets who teach* (pp. 15–16). New York, NY: HarperCollins.

ABOUT THE AUTHOR

Todd Stanley is author of many teacher education books, including *Project-Based Learning for Gifted Students: A Handbook for the 21st-Century Classroom* and *Performance-Based Assessment for 21st-Century Skills*. He was a classroom teacher for 18 years, teaching students as young as second graders and as old as high school seniors, and was a National Board Certified teacher. He helped create a gifted academy for grades 5–8, which employs inquiry-based learning, project-based learning, and performance-based assessment. He is currently the gifted services coordinator for Pickerington Local School District in Ohio, where he lives with his wife, Nicki, and two daughters, Anna and Abby. You can follow him on Twitter @the_gifted_guy or visit his website at https://www.thegiftedguy.com.

NEXT GENERATION SCIENCE STANDARDS ALIGNMENT

Project	Next Generation Science Standards
Project 1	3-5-ETS1-1. Define a simple design problem reflecting a need or a want that includes specified criteria for success and constraints on materials, time, or cost.
Project 2	3-5-ETS1-1. Define a simple design problem reflecting a need or a want that includes specified criteria for success and constraints on materials, time, or cost.
	3-5-ETS1-2. Generate and compare multiple possible solutions to a problem based on how well each is likely to meet the criteria and constraints of the problem.
	3-5-ETS1-3. Plan and carry out fair tests in which variables are controlled and failure points are considered to identify aspects of a model or prototype that can be improved.
Project 3	*Note*. Standards for this project will vary based upon students' selected topics.
Project 6	3-5-ETS1-1. Define a simple design problem reflecting a need or a want that includes specified criteria for success and constraints on materials, time, or cost.
Project 8	3-5-ETS1-1. Define a simple design problem reflecting a need or a want that includes specified criteria for success and constraints on materials, time, or cost.

Project	Next Generation Science Standards
Project 8, *continued*	3-5-ETS1-2. Generate and compare multiple possible solutions to a problem based on how well each is likely to meet the criteria and constraints of the problem.
	3-5-ETS1-3. Plan and carry out fair tests in which variables are controlled and failure points are considered to identify aspects of a model or prototype that can be improved.
Project 9	*Note.* Standards for this project will vary based upon students' selected topics.

COMMON CORE STATE STANDARDS ALIGNMENT

Project	Subject	Standards
Project 1	ELA	RL.4.5 Explain major differences between poems, drama, and prose, and refer to the structural elements of poems (e.g., verse, rhythm, meter) and drama (e.g., casts of characters, settings, descriptions, dialogue, stage directions) when writing or speaking about a text.
		W.4.4 Produce clear and coherent writing in which the development and organization are appropriate to task, purpose, and audience.
		RL.5.5 Explain how a series of chapters, scenes, or stanzas fits together to provide the overall structure of a particular story, drama, or poem.
		W.5.4 Produce clear and coherent writing in which the development and organization are appropriate to task, purpose, and audience.
Project 2	Math	4.MD.A Solve problems involving measurement and conversion of measurements.
		4.MD.B Represent and interpret data.
		4.MD.C Geometric measurement: understand concepts of angle and measure angles.
		5.MD.B Represent and interpret data.

Project	Subject	Standards
Project 3	ELA	RI.4.3 Explain events, procedures, ideas, or concepts in a historical, scientific, or technical text, including what happened and why, based on specific information in the text.
		RI.4.4 Determine the meaning of general academic and domain-specific words or phrases in a text relevant to a grade 4 topic or subject area.
		RI.4.7 Interpret information presented visually, orally, or quantitatively (e.g., in charts, graphs, diagrams, time lines, animations, or interactive elements on Web pages) and explain how the information contributes to an understanding of the text in which it appears.
		RI.4.9 Integrate information from two texts on the same topic in order to write or speak about the subject knowledgeably.
		W.4.2 Write informative/explanatory texts to examine a topic and convey ideas and information clearly.
		W.4.4 Produce clear and coherent writing in which the development and organization are appropriate to task, purpose, and audience.
		W.4.7 Conduct short research projects that build knowledge through investigation of different aspects of a topic.
		W.4.8 Recall relevant information from experiences or gather relevant information from print and digital sources; take notes and categorize information, and provide a list of sources.
		SL.4.4 Report on a topic or text, tell a story, or recount an experience in an organized manner, using appropriate facts and relevant, descriptive details to support main ideas or themes; speak clearly at an understandable pace.

Project	Subject	Standards
Project 3, *continued*	ELA, *continued*	SL.4.5 Add audio recordings and visual displays to presentations when appropriate to enhance the development of main ideas or themes.
		RI.5.7 Draw on information from multiple print or digital sources, demonstrating the ability to locate an answer to a question quickly or to solve a problem efficiently.
		RI.5.9 Integrate information from several texts on the same topic in order to write or speak about the subject knowledgeably.
		W.5.2 Write informative/explanatory texts to examine a topic and convey ideas and information clearly.
		W.5.4 Produce clear and coherent writing in which the development and organization are appropriate to task, purpose, and audience.
		W.5.7 Conduct short research projects that use several sources to build knowledge through investigation of different aspects of a topic.
		W.5.8 Recall relevant information from experiences or gather relevant information from print and digital sources; summarize or paraphrase information in notes and finished work, and provide a list of sources.
		SL.5.4 Report on a topic or text or present an opinion, sequencing ideas logically and using appropriate facts and relevant, descriptive details to support main ideas or themes; speak clearly at an understandable pace.
		SL.5.5 Include multimedia components (e.g., graphics, sound) and visual displays in presentations when appropriate to enhance the development of main ideas or themes.
	Math	*Note*. Standards for this project will vary based upon students' selected topics.

Project	Subject	Standards
Project 4	Math	4.MD.B Represent and interpret data.
		5.MD.B Represent and interpret data.
Project 5	Math	*Note.* Standards for this project will vary based upon students' selected topics.
Project 6	ELA	W.4.7 Conduct short research projects that build knowledge through investigation of different aspects of a topic.
		SL.4.4 Report on a topic or text, tell a story, or recount an experience in an organized manner, using appropriate facts and relevant, descriptive details to support main ideas or themes; speak clearly at an understandable pace.
		W.5.7 Conduct short research projects that use several sources to build knowledge through investigation of different aspects of a topic.
		SL.5.4 Report on a topic or text or present an opinion, sequencing ideas logically and using appropriate facts and relevant, descriptive details to support main ideas or themes; speak clearly at an understandable pace.
Project 7	Math	4.OA.C Generate and analyze patterns.
		4.MD.B Represent and interpret data.
		5.OA.A Write and interpret numerical expressions.
		5.OA.B Analyze patterns and relationships.
		5.MD.B Represent and interpret data.
Project 9	ELA	W.4.7 Conduct short research projects that build knowledge through investigation of different aspects of a topic.
		SL.4.4 Report on a topic or text, tell a story, or recount an experience in an organized manner, using appropriate facts and relevant, descriptive details to support main ideas or themes; speak clearly at an understandable pace.

<table>
<tr><th>Project</th><th>Subject</th><th>Standards</th></tr>
<tr><td rowspan="2">Project 9, continued</td><td rowspan="2">ELA, continued</td><td>W.5.7 Conduct short research projects that use several sources to build knowledge through investigation of different aspects of a topic.</td></tr>
<tr><td>SL.5.4 Report on a topic or text or present an opinion, sequencing ideas logically and using appropriate facts and relevant, descriptive details to support main ideas or themes; speak clearly at an understandable pace.</td></tr>
<tr><td rowspan="5">Project 10</td><td rowspan="4">ELA</td><td>W.4.2 Write informative/explanatory texts to examine a topic and convey ideas and information clearly.</td></tr>
<tr><td>W.4.4 Produce clear and coherent writing in which the development and organization are appropriate to task, purpose, and audience.</td></tr>
<tr><td>W.5.2 Write informative/explanatory texts to examine a topic and convey ideas and information clearly.</td></tr>
<tr><td>W.5.4 Produce clear and coherent writing in which the development and organization are appropriate to task, purpose, and audience.</td></tr>
<tr><td>Math</td><td>Note. Standards for this project will vary based upon students' selected topics.</td></tr>
</table>